reality**check**

the student's guide to the real world

grantbaldwin

Published by Priority Productions
Springfield, Missouri

Library of Congress Control Number: 2008930555
ISBN: 978-0-9818558-0-6

Published by Priority Productions, Missouri

Printed in the United States of America

Cover design and layout by Kelsey Davajon
kdavajon@gmail.com

Sixth Printing

This book is dedicated to my best friend, my partner, my wife.
Thanks for your love and unconditional support.
I love you Sheila.

acknowledgements

Writing this book has been a journey, and journeys are best taken with others. I couldn't have done this project without the support of so many people.

Mom – I've heard it said, "No one loves his mother more than Grant does!" And it's true. Your influence in my life is evident every day. Thank you for believing in me, for pushing me to dream, and for your love and support. Oh, and thanks for letting me use your house for writing this book!

Dad – You've taught me to work hard for what I want in life and to create my own destiny. This book is evidence of not only the incredible father that you've been, but also the values that you've helped to instill into my life. So I guess this book is partly your fault!

Taylor & Kelsey – I'm truly grateful to have such amazing siblings like yourselves. Yes, you read that correctly. I'm thankful for you both. Thank you for your editing feedback and input on this project. And thanks to Kelsey for all the design and formatting work you put into this book. You really made this book look good!

I have countless friends, family, and mentors that have helped shape the person that I am today. I value, respect, and love each one of you. You know who you are. Thanks for believing in someone like me.

Thank you to the students who I have met from across the country who have allowed me to speak into your lives. And especially to the numerous students who read through sections of this project and have helped shape this book. Special thanks to Alison, Beau, Billy, Brooke, Casey, Danielle, David, Haleigh, Jarrod, Kelly, Laymon, Levi, Matt, Rochelle, and Tara. Also, thanks to Marsha Yalden for adding an English teacher's touch. Finally, thanks to my friend and general manager, Lisa Klug, who keeps me organized and makes my life easy!

Sydnee, Emilee & Mylee - I absolutely adore all of you and am honored to be your daddy. Thanks for allowing me to travel around and run my mouth, and for being sweet to Mommy while I'm away. You girls remind me daily of what matters most in life, and why I do what I do.

Sheila – You are everything I could ever hope for in a wife. You allow me to dream big dreams and support me through the ups and downs of it all. Thank you for your patience, your grace, your advice, your support, your encouragement, and your love. I couldn't do this without you. Thanks, Pal.

Finally, I'd also like to thank the Academy for this award.

And Live from New York...It's Saturday Night...

table of contents

table of contents

You've waited for this moment your entire life. The moment when you can spread your wings, leave the nest, and try to fly. You've dreamed about growing up, living on your own, and being an adult in the real world. You're counting down the days until you will have the freedom to come and go as you please, to eat what you want when you want, and to listen to your music as loud as you'd like. You imagine having your own bathroom that you don't have to share with your disgusting siblings, not having to eat Mom's mystery meat anymore, and going to Wal-Mart at 3am just because you can.

I'm sure by now you frequently remind your parents how many days they have left in your presence before you will be departing for greener pastures. You imagine how distraught they will be, weeping with emotion as you drive away from the house (only to later learn they had a party when you left). The air is filled with excitement, anxiety, enthusiasm, and anticipation as you grow up and prepare to enter the real world. But then it hits you like a ton of bricks...

A Reality Check.

The days of choosing between white milk and chocolate milk with your cookies are replaced by paying bills, making career decisions, attending college classes, and doing your taxes. Recess and nap time are distant memories that have now been exchanged for frustrations with your boss, relationship challenges, and the need for health insurance. Pretty exciting, huh?

Don't get me wrong. Growing up is just part of life, and this new chapter that you're entering into is one of the most exciting times that you'll ever experience. But if you're like most students, you have a mountain of unanswered questions about what to do next. When you think about it, life has been a pretty simple and steady routine up to this point. You've always been told where to go, what time to be there, when to sit, when to stand, and how to avoid making a fool of yourself in public. And while many of those concepts still apply to this new chapter of life, there is still so much that just seems unclear.

It's all incredibly thrilling, but it also feels incredibly overwhelming. You teeter between the feeling of "I can't wait to get there," and the emotion that says "I miss my Mommy!" That feeling that you're experiencing is one felt by every other student who has been in your position. You're not the first one to feel that way, and you definitely won't be the last. You're experiencing something far too common...

A Reality Check.

So where do you begin to get the answers that you're looking for about this transition to life in the real world? You probably have questions about choosing a college, preparing for marriage, moving away from friends, finding a place to live, making a budget, and living a balanced life. Plus the hundreds of other questions, cares, and concerns that race through your head.

Well, you've come to the right place, and hopefully I can help. Since we're going to be hanging out together for the next several pages, let me introduce myself. My name is Grant, and I've spent a good chunk of my life trying to motivate, inspire, encourage, and equip students just like you. Maybe I'm strange (well I know I am), but I actually really like students. While most adults find it easy to look down upon and criticize "young people" today, they may have forgotten that they were your age once. Clearly the old age and lack of memory is affecting them.

But we've all been in your shoes before with the "deer in the headlights look," trying to figure out what to do next. I know I've been there. But at the same time, I can think of numerous people in my life who have helped me to make the transition into the person I am today. And I hope, in some small way, that this book is able to do that for you.

As you may have already noticed, this book is broken down into five main sections that address the common issues and questions that students have about entering into the real world. I cover issues related to college, relationships, money, life in the real world, and several deeper questions that you may be asking. Also, I think it's important you know I didn't just pull out a bunch of random questions for this book. I spent several months interviewing and talking with teenagers like you from around the country, and I asked them what questions they were looking for answers to. It was based on their feedback and questions that this book was formed.

While you can certainly read this book in sequential order, you can also feel free to skip around and read about the most pressing questions in your life right now. There will be some questions that may not apply to you today but could come up in a few months or years. There are other questions that perhaps you've already answered in life but you may need to refer back to in the future. This resource is *your* resource. My hope is that this book becomes a valuable resource to you, and that you are able to refer to it for direction and guidance on a regular basis. This is your book so utilize it how it makes the most sense for you.

Regardless of the order you read this book in, I will ask you to do one thing up front. I'm going to ask you to commit to do something differently in your life as a result of what you read.

Part of the value of books and learning in general is that they allow us the opportunity to implement and apply new ideas to our lives. Far too often, something is just a "nice idea," and we can see the value of applying it, but we never actually do anything with it. So as you read this book, I would challenge you to continue to ask yourself a simple two-word question: Now What? What are you going to do differently as a result of what you're reading?

Having said that, I will give you a little disclaimer about this book. I don't want to disappoint you, but this book contains no magic formula, secret pill, or special sauce for helping you to transition into the real world. Few things in life come with a simple solution, an easy explanation, or a quick fix answer. Life in the real world is a blast, but it certainly has its share of challenges. Although I may or may not have ever met you, I know that you can be successful. I know that you're smart enough to realize that success doesn't just happen. It's something that you have to work at on a continual basis.

I wrote this book because not only do I love working with students, but because I believe in students. I believe that you can live the dream you desire. I know I am. Is it easy? Of course not. Is it worth it? Absolutely. But it starts with...

A Reality Check.

section one

college:
i miss kindergarten

chapter one
should I go to college?

As we dive into this question, it is important to note that when we talk about going to college, we are talking about more than just a traditional four-year institution. For you, college may be getting your two-year associates degree at a local community college. It may be going to a technical school. Perhaps it is studying a particular trade or skill such as cosmetology or massage therapy. So know that when we talk about "college," it means a lot of different things to a lot of different people. Now back to our original question!

I guess the easy answer would be, "Of course, you should go to college!" But to be honest, I would have to disagree with that blanket statement. The question, "Should I go to college," is one of those 30,000-foot questions that is easy to have a knee-jerk, common sense answer for, but the truth is that it depends on you. You should go to college if it *makes sense* for you to go to college.

Don't get me wrong. There are plenty of statistics to support someone going to college:

• The Census Bureau estimates that someone with a two-year degree will earn on average $500,000 more over the course of their lifetime than someone with just a high school diploma. Someone with a four-year degree will earn on average $1 million more over the course of his/her lifetime than someone with just a high school education.[1]

• College graduates made an average of $51,554 in 2004 (the most recent figures available), compared with $28,645 for adults with a high school diploma. High school drop-outs earned an average of $19,169, and those with advanced college degrees made an average of $78,093.[2]

On top of that, many potential employers won't even consider you unless you have a college degree. In many cases, they may not be as concerned with what your major or degree was in as long as you have one. By having a college degree, regardless of what it is for, you show an employer that you have what it takes to be disciplined, work hard, and accomplish a goal.

But the question of whether or not you should go to college has a lot of stereotypes and myths associated with it. So let's separate some fact from fiction:

myth:
"You can't be successful unless you have a college degree."
truth:
A lot of successful people in the world don't have college degrees.

Let me give you a few names, and based on their success, you tell me which of these individuals have a college degree:

• Michael Dell – started and runs Dell Inc., one of the most profitable PC manufacturers in the world.

• Walt Disney – theme parks, movies, cartoons...he started all that!

• Henry Ford – started Ford Motor Company and revolutionized the automobile industry.

• Bill Gates – the founder of Microsoft and the world's richest person...not bad.

• Steve Jobs – if you're a Mac fan, chances are you have an iPod, an iPhone, or a MacBook. He co-founded Apple.

Would you be surprised if I told you that none of them have a college degree? While some of them may have gone to college for a couple of semesters and others may have never even started in the first place, not one of these individuals has a college degree. And yet in the eyes of our culture, we would consider them to be "successful." At the same time, it is important to note that all of these people did not get a traditional job like what you may be looking for. Rather, they each started businesses that have gone on to become some of the largest and most successful organizations in history.

myth:
"I need a degree to fall back on."
truth:
A college degree is no guarantee for a great career.

Having a college degree in your pocket to "fall back on" is a pretty expensive Plan-B! Why would you spend the money to get a degree for something that you may or may not use in the future? In fact, according to the U.S. Bureau of Labor Statistics, eight of the top 10 fastest-growing occupations through 2014 do not require a bachelor's degree.[3]

Think about it this way. How many stay-at-home moms and dads are there that have college degrees? I'm not against staying home to raise children. (I'm actually really for it. My wife is a stay-at-home mom.) But doesn't it seem silly to spend thousands and thousands of dollars on a college degree if you plan on staying home? It just seems logical to get a degree when you actually need it, or when you can see a direct return on your investment.

myth:
"The more degrees I have, the more money I'll make."
truth:
You can have a lot of degrees and still be lousy at what you do.

You may know people like this who assume that if they have a lot of degrees, employers have no choice but to pay them a lot of money! And while it's true that in some industries, you will get a pay raise with a graduate level degree, this is not always the case. If you have seven different degrees from a bunch of prestigious universities, but if you are an unproductive worker, or you are just a jerk to work with, how valuable do you think those degrees really are?

"So Grant, you seem kind of against college?" I'm sure these ideas may give that impression, but nothing could be further from the truth. I went to college and graduated with a bachelor's degree and have a pretty piece of paper with my name on it to prove it. My point is that the pretty piece of paper doesn't guarantee that I will be successful, nor does it assure me that I'll make more money than someone without a degree. A degree gives you no promises or guarantees other than what you do with the knowledge you obtained. And that part is up to you.

Having said that, going to college and getting a degree of some kind makes sense for most people. Years and years ago, when many of the primary industries in our country were based out of factories, people were paid based on how many widgets or doodads they could produce on an assembly line. In today's culture and work environment, you are paid based on not only what you know, but what you do with that knowledge. And obviously one of the leading sources for gaining knowledge and education is through colleges and universities.

are the ACT and SAT really that important?

Scantrons. Number 2 Pencils. Multiple Choice. If you're like most students, all of these images cause fear, trembling, and many sleepless nights. So if this describes you, be encouraged... you're normal.

The answer to this question is really yes and no. Colleges and universities will use ACT and SAT scores in two primary ways: admissions and scholarships. But beyond this broad generality, how schools will use your test scores becomes more of an art than a science! Although it seems like there is no rhyme or reason to the process, most schools will place at least some value on what your scores are. So let's break down the two ways that these scores are used.

admissions

Most schools will look at your overall performance as a student when determining whether or not you will be accepted, so your test scores will be one part of that equation. To some schools, your test scores may make or break you. Different schools will view these tests in different ways, so it is always a good idea to talk with the admissions office of the schools you are interested in to make sure you know the value they place on these tests.

Most schools will now accept both ACT and SAT test results, but it's always a good idea to check with schools first to see if they have a preference. Generally speaking, the more selective the school, the more important your ACT or SAT scores will be. In addition, the ACT is typically used more in Midwest schools and the SAT is generally used more in coastal schools.

Because each school will use these scores in different ways, this gives you, the student, a strategic advantage. Let mc explain what I mean. While both are widely accepted standardized tests, the ACT and SAT are considerably different types of tests. Because of this, you may do extremely well on one test but completely bomb the other.

This happens because, in reality, each tost measures different skills. Kaplan, a great resource for preparing for either of these tests, says this: "Admissions officers and educators often describe the difference between the ACT and the SAT in these terms: the ACT is a content-based test, whereas the SAT tests critical thinking and problem solving."[1] Because each test rewards different skills, it may simply come down to which kind best suits your test-taking abilities.

Here are a few items to consider that show how the ACT and SAT are very different:[2]

- The ACT has a science reasoning test; the SAT does not.
- The ACT math section has trigonometry; the SAT does not.
- The SAT tests vocabulary much more than the ACT.
- The SAT is not entirely multiple choice; the ACT is.
- The SAT has a guessing penalty; the ACT does not.
- The ACT tests English grammar; the SAT does not.

scholarships
The other primary way that ACT and SAT scores are used is in determining scholarship recipients. In reality, this may be one of the biggest criteria for determining not only whether you receive a certain scholarship, but also how much money you might get.

Think about it from the perspective of a scholarship committee. Let's say you have 10 scholarships to pass out worth a total of $100,000 and you have 200 students to choose from. These 200 students are from 200 different schools from different cities around the country and all over the world. They all have outstanding applications listing off their accomplishments, community involvement, GPA, plus a stack of quality recommendation letters. You can see that it might be very difficult to compare apples to apples when determining who to give the scholarships to.

So what is one of the best ways to "level the playing field"? You guessed it.

Dodge Ball Tournament.

The other option would, of course, be to compare your ACT or SAT scores. (But a dodge ball tournament would sure make it interesting.) The Admissions Director at one major university in the Midwest said while every school is different, they have found that ACT and SAT test scores are more important in determining scholarships than in determining acceptance into the school.

Now maybe you are a student who is extremely intelligent, but you just aren't the best when it comes to taking a test. There are two main things you can consider. One, do any kind of prep work necessary to prepare for this test. You may want to take a practice exam, try sample questions, or even hire a tutor specifically to prepare for taking the ACT or SAT. The second thing you might want to consider is the growing number of schools that do not require either test for acceptance. At www.fairtest.org, you can find a list of over 750 four-year colleges that do not use the ACT or SAT to admit applicants.

The bottom line is every school is different, so take the time to ask questions and find out how important the ACT and SAT is to them. Talk not only to the admissions office, but also with those in charge of scholarships. Because both the ACT and SAT tests are only offered a few times each year, you may be better off to go ahead and take one or maybe both tests just to be on the safe side. If you are going to take one of the tests, take the time to study and prepare for it, and make it worth your time. Who knows? You may end up with a $5,000 scholarship! That would make your mom proud.

how do I find the right college for me?

As you may have already figured out, finding that one perfect school is not the easiest thing in the world to do. There are literally thousands of options available ranging from public schools to private schools; technical schools to community colleges; four-year programs and two-year plans; plus in-state and out-of-state universities. I'm sure sometimes you feel like just throwing a dart at a map and finding a school wherever it lands! Or the classic "eeney-meeney-miney-mo" is also a possible method for selection. But when it comes down to finding a college that is right for you, here are a few things to consider:

location
For some students, they want to be as close to home as possible, and for other students, they want to know how far from home they can possibly get! However, don't discount where the school is located. Would you rather be in a major metropolitan area or would you prefer a quieter, small-town feel? When considering geographic location, it is also good to consider the cost-of-living for a particular area. That may be a determining factor if you really want to live there.

cost

There are two primary schools of thought when it comes to choosing a college based on cost. One approach is that you should never rule out a college you are truly interested in based on cost alone, because you may be eligible for a lot of scholarships and grants that can help offset the expense. The other way of thinking is that you really shouldn't bite off more than you can chew financially. I tend to lean more towards the second school of thought. While I wouldn't deny that some schools may offer better educational opportunities, you have to ask yourself if it is really *that* much better to justify the extra expense. I think you would find that the majority of the time, it is not.

size

Some students are looking for a major university experience with 30,000+ students, while others prefer a smaller setting with only a few hundred students. Either option is fine, but you have to choose which makes sense for you. There are trade-offs either way you go. You can go to a huge state school and have an endless amount of opportunities and options, but the downside is that you're just another student in what really feels like a small city. On the other side of the coin, you can go to a smaller, local college and have more personal attention from the professors and meet more people on campus. The downside is that the clubs and extracurricular activities may be more limited.

academic options

Finally, you want to find a school that is strong in your particular field of interest. If you want to be an architect, look up the top 25 rated architecture schools and see how they each stack up to the other criteria that are important to you. If you're not entirely sure what you want to do when you graduate from college, you will want to look for schools that offer a well-rounded educational experience with a wide variety of majors and minors.

Once you have a list of about ten schools you are really interested in, you can begin to narrow down that list to about five that you think are worth a visit. A campus visit is basically a chance for you to do a "test drive" and see what the school and campus are really like. Take the time to review websites for various colleges, talk with your high school counselor about the schools you are interested in, and contact the colleges to learn all you can about that school.

Here are some additional resources that may help you with this process:

www.fastweb.com
They have great resources for finding colleges and scholarships.

www.mycollegeoptions.com
This is a free personalized college matching service.

This is **your** future, and it's **your** responsibility to prepare for it.

how do I apply for college?

Applying for college is a process that you definitely need to be familiar with. So let's walk through a few things to consider that will make this procedure a little easier:

understand the process
Unfortunately, applying to college has become a little more than filling out a form or two. While paperwork (and plenty of it) is certainly part of the process, it is only one piece of the bigger puzzle. In order to really begin to understand the application and admissions process, you have to understand some common terms.

deferred
If you've been deferred, it simply means you will not receive a final decision from the school for another few months. It isn't a "no," but it's not quite a "maybe" either.

early decision
This is a good option if you know 100% for sure where you want to go to college. Colleges typically won't allow application materials before a certain date, but early decision means you

can send them in before that date and receive an immediate decision. The downside is that if you go this route, it is generally considered a binding agreement, and you will have to attend that school. With early decision you're saying, "If I get in, I'm going there."

open admissions

This is common among community colleges because you are generally assured admittance regardless of your educational credentials.

restrictive early action

This is similar to the Early Decision process. The main difference is that while you still get to apply early, you get a non-binding decision which allows you to still apply to other schools.

rolling admissions

Some schools offer rolling admissions which means that they generally don't have a set deadline for when you need to apply. Because of this, it is somewhat of a "first-come, first-serve" basis, although you still may need to meet certain application and admissions requirements.

wait-listed

Being wait-listed falls into the category of a "maybe" answer. It is like being on a wait list at a restaurant. You may have to wait quite a while for a table, and, in some cases, you may never even get a table. You can choose to wait and hope you make it in, but if you're smart about it, you should go ahead and begin establishing a backup plan.

know what colleges look for

Understanding what colleges are looking for in their students seems more like an art than a science. Some schools accept a large percentage of students, and other highly selective schools may only accept a small handful of applicants. For example, Yale University registered one of the lowest rate of admissions for the class of 2008, only admitting 9.9% of applicants, 1,950 students in total from the 19,674 students who applied.[1]

Most schools will generally look at the "numbers" first. By "numbers," I mean they want to see your grades, your class rank, your ACT or SAT scores, and how challenging your class load was in high school. While it may be fun to take P.E. all day, every day, colleges frown on that. Shocking, I know. Again, understand that every school is different, but, for many colleges today, if your "numbers" are good enough, they will go ahead and accept you. If your "numbers" are a little shaky, they may need some additional information to make a decision. This could be a case where you are "deferred" or "wait-listed" as I mentioned above.

Beyond the "numbers," schools looking for additional information about you, or schools that are highly selective, may also want an essay from you or usually some letters of recommendation. You want to get recommendation letters from those people who know you best, and, honestly, if they have a fancy job title, it can help as well! In order to really understand what a school is looking for, one of the most effective methods is just to call their admissions office and ask. Tell them you're a prospective student and that you're trying to figure out some key things their school is really looking for in their students.

Also, be aware of information that may end up as part of your application without you even knowing about it. A growing number of colleges are doing background checks and online checks. They google your name, and look up your blogs, your web pages, and your profiles on social networking sites. My advice is if you don't want it ending up in your college application, you may not want to put it on the internet. It may be a good idea to put this book down for a second (only a second) and take that picture down from your site.

Last, but not least, make sure you utilize your school counselors. Their job is to help set you up for success after you graduate.

Ask them questions, pick their brains, and tap the wealth of information that they provide. But remember, while they are there to help and be a resource for you, they are not there to do everything for you or hold your hand through the entire process. As you get ready to graduate, remember that you're becoming an adult (I know that sounds crazy), and it is your responsibility to stay on top of the process. Don't get sloppy, miss deadlines, or assume your counselor or your parents will take care of it. This is your future, and It's *your* responsibility to prepare for it.

how am I going to pay for college?

When we were younger (and maybe more naïve), we really didn't have to think much about this question; did we? We just assumed that college would somehow magically pay for itself. Maybe from our parents or from the government or perhaps if we racked up enough quarters from the tooth fairy, we could pay for school. But the danger is that most students today start school without ever taking the time to answer this question.

One of the best things you can do as a teenager is take the time to think this through before you actually go to college. Otherwise, you may look up in four years and find yourself with an entry-level job and a very expensive school bill that needs to be paid. Consider these statistics:

• The National Center for Education Statistics found the average college graduate in 2003-04 owed $19,000 in student loans after four years of college. For law and medical school students, that amount could easily end up being six-figures.[1]

• Over the past decade, debt levels for graduating seniors with student loans more than doubled from $9,250 to $19,200 – a 108% increase.[2]

• In 2004, nearly two-thirds (62.4%) of graduates from public universities had student loans.[3]

The inaccurate perception is that student loan debt is okay because you are investing in education. But if you graduate from college with several thousand dollars in student loan debt and no way to pay it off, that's a bad start to the real world. While student loans aren't necessarily a horrible option, they do have a tendency to linger with you long after you graduate. With that in mind, let's explore other options beyond loans to help pay for college:

FAFSA (Free Application for Federal Student Aid)
This is the single largest source of financial aid available, so you definitely need to fill out this form. You will want to fill it out each year you are in college, and it must be signed by your parents. The government will use this information to determine your eligibility for federal student aid including Pell grants, Stafford loans, PLUS loans, and work-study programs.

scholarships
We will talk more about scholarships in the next chapter, but take the time to apply for as many as possible. Put it this way: if it takes you an hour to apply, and you get a $500 scholarship as a result, that's a pretty good payday considering how little time you put into it! Last time I checked, McDonald's wasn't paying $500 per hour.

community colleges
You might consider getting your general education classes (math, reading, history, science, etc.) knocked out at a local community college. You will almost always find it to be much less expensive, and the classes can often transfer to a "better" school that you are interested in attending later. I did this for two semesters in college, and it saved me thousands of dollars. Be sure to check with the school you want to attend later to make sure the community college classes you are planning on taking will transfer.

work study programs
Many colleges offer some type of work study program that you can have a part-time job on campus that helps contribute towards the cost of your education. Check with the financial aid office of the college you are interested in to see what kind of work study options they have available for students.

AP & CLEP tests
These are two great ways to earn college credit and save money while still in high school. AP (Advanced Placement) and CLEP (College Level Examination Program) are programs that allow you the opportunity to receive college credit for what you already know by earning qualifying scores on various tests. Consider the path taken by Meghan Price of Gainesville, Georgia. Because she scored well on the six AP subject exams she took in high school, she was able to enroll as a college sophomore for her first year at the University of Massachusetts in Boston. By spending three years on campus instead of four, she will save between $32,000 and $34,000.[4]

live at home
While I certainly understand that you are counting down the days until you can move out, I would encourage you to slow down a little bit. I know that living on your own seems awesome (and most days it is!), but it also brings with it a new set of financial responsibilities. While there is nothing wrong with wanting to live on campus to experience dorm life, you can literally save yourself thousands of dollars by living at home during a few semesters of your college years.

While college is a pretty good investment, it can definitely be expensive. But there are certainly ways to minimize what that expense will be. Begin now to financially plan for college tomorrow, so you don't get stuck paying for it for the rest of your life.

free money? scholarships? grants? where do I find that?

I think we would all agree that the best kind of money is free money! As you prepare to go to college, and create your game plan to pay for it (you did just read the last chapter, right?), a smart strategy is to find as much free money as possible. It almost seems too easy, doesn't it?! While getting scholarships and grants for college isn't extremely difficult, it does require a major investment on your part: time. You have to take the time to not only find the scholarships and grants that you are eligible for, but also take the time to apply for them. Remember, this investment of time has the potential to earn you some serious cash to help pay for school.

You have to understand up front that finding and applying for "free money" is hard work, but it can be done, and it is definitely worth your time. For example, did you know that there were $63 billion in grants and scholarships awarded last year? You read correctly...that's BILLION with a 'B!' That is a lot of money available! So how do you get your hands on some of this money? Three simple steps...

find it

Think of it like you are mining for gold, or that you're a bargain hunter who has to browse through piles of items to find the buried treasure you're looking for. While it may seem overwhelming, remember it's worth the time. In order to find scholarships, you have to understand what they are given out for. Scholarships are given out for a variety of reasons ranging from the major categories of academics, athletics, and interests, to other categories such as your parent's employer, community involvement, and ethnicity. How do you find scholarships? Here are some ways:

online

There are tons of scholarship searches online that are worth your time to look into. When looking online, remember this one principle: never ever, ever, ever pay for a scholarship search. I don't care if they offer you a new car; it's not worth it. There are a lot of scams out there that will make plenty of empty promises. Here is a list of reputable scholarship search sites that are free:

www.fastweb.com
www.petersons.com
www.scholarshipexperts.com
www.scholarships.com
www.findtuition.com
www.collegeboard.com

your college

Talk to the college you're interested in to see what types of scholarships the school offers, and what you need to do to qualify. The vast majority of scholarships awarded come directly from individual colleges and universities.

corporations

Almost all of the major corporations you've heard of and whose products you use offer scholarships. From Coca-Cola to Microsoft to Dell, they all have scholarships available. For them, it is an opportunity to not only advertise their brand but also to possibly attract future employees to their company.

local businesses

Realistically, you may have a better chance earning a scholarship from a local company than from a national corporation, but it is smart to check both options. If you know what field you plan on going into, call local businesses in that industry to see if they offer any scholarships, or if they would be willing to help fund any of your education.

area clubs & groups

There are several local civic groups and organizations in your area that offer scholarships. Groups like Rotary Clubs, Lion's Club, and Jaycees all offer scholarships. Visit your Chamber of Commerce, browse the phone book, and scan your local newspaper to find some of these local groups.

professional associations

Just like the strategy for working with local businesses, if you know what type of work you want to pursue, look into the various professional associations to see what kinds of scholarships they offer to students going into that field. Associations for journalism, engineering, psychology, and marketing are just a few of the many industry organizations that can provide you with scholarship options.

religious institutions

Check not only with your own church but also with other area churches. While some require you be a member, others just want to help support area youth, so it never hurts to ask.

your parents

I don't mean ask your parents if they will offer you a scholarship! They've already provided you a scholarship for most of your life by letting you eat their food and live in their house! Rather, check with your parents' employers or labor unions to see if they offer scholarships to children of their employees. Also, ask if any of the clubs and organizations they belong to offer scholarships.

apply for it

Once you have found the scholarships you may qualify for, then you have to let the sponsors know you want that money! Here are some ideas when applying:

every application is different

Some are just a simple one page form you have to fill out. Others require an essay, recommendation letters, and the rights to name your first born child. Not really...at least, not that I'm aware of. So just make sure you know exactly what you need to do to apply. Some scholarship application requirements are so strict that if you don't turn in everything required, you're automatically disqualified from the scholarship. Ouch!

every dollar matters

It is easy to overlook the $250 and $500 scholarships because they don't seem worth your time. However, because many students think of it this way, you may have a better chance of getting these scholarships. With that mindset, fewer might apply, which would increase your chances of getting the money.

it's a numbers game

To some degree, applying for scholarships is a numbers game. You're smart enough to know that the more scholarships you apply for, the more likely you'll be to receive some. But that also means being strategic and figuring out which ones best fit you and your qualifications.

spend it wisely

Every scholarship is different, so make sure you know exactly what each one is for. Some scholarships are open-ended, and may be spent on whatever educational expenses you have, ranging from tuition to books to fees to that "research trip" to the Bahamas! Others are a little more specific and may be used for only certain expenses. On top of that, find out if the scholarship is a one-time award or if it is renewable, which means you could receive that scholarship each year you are in college. If it is renewable, make sure you know what you need to do to keep getting the money. Do you need to maintain a certain GPA? What happens if you change your major? Do you have to stay involved with a particular group or organization? Make sure you know all the details, so you spend that money wisely.

Finding and applying for scholarships isn't brain surgery (although you definitely need scholarships if you're going to be a brain surgeon!), but it does require time and hard work. Look at it this way: if you don't get that scholarship now, you're going to have to either earn the money by working a part time job (for $8 an hour) or borrow it and pay it back at a crazy interest rate. Personally, I'd rather spend the time now and get the free money that's available.

chapter seven
what classes should I take to prepare for my future career?

In college, just like in most high school settings, you basically have two types of classes: general education and electives. You're going to have a variety of general education classes (commonly called gen-ed classes) that will be required. These classes are for the typical primary subjects such as math, science, history, English, writing, etc. Often times, your major will determine which of these classes are required and at what levels. For example, if you are an accounting major, you will probably have several gen-ed math classes since you're going to be working closely with numbers. If you are a journalism major, you may not have as many math classes, but you may have several writing classes. The number and the type of gen-ed classes you will be required to take will typically be determined by your major.

After that, you have electives. These are the classes that you are probably really looking forward to. It is in these classes where you begin to really dive in and learn about the specifics of your career path. Going back to our example of an accountant, after taking some gen-ed level math classes, you may have more specific electives such as Tax Accounting, Accounting Concepts for Managers, or Accounting for Non-

Profit Organizations. When it comes to which elective classes you will take, you will have some choice but a number of your electives will be determined by your major. Your major may have several different elective classes you must take to fulfill certain requirements, but you may also have a list of additional electives to choose from. As an example, in order to meet the requirements of your major, you may also have to take four classes of your choice from a list of ten class options.

Most majors have a large variety of electives to help you further hone in on what you want to do. If you want to be an accountant, do you want to manage the finances of a large company, or would you rather help individuals with their taxes? Do you want to work for the IRS or do you prefer to help small business owners with their day-to-day financial operations?

actual classes at american colleges

If you're really looking for a class to stretch you, look into attending some of these:

Philosophy & Star Trek
Georgetown University

Daytime Serials: Family & Social Roles
University of Wisconsin

The American Vacation
University of Iowa

Horror Film in Context
Bowdoin College

Comparative History of Organized Crime
Williams College

The Art of Sin & the Sin of Art
Rhode Island School of Design

The Art of Walking
Centre College

Death & the 19th Century
Purdue University

The Science of Harry Potter
Frostburg State University

The Simpsons as Social Science
San Jose State

Once you figure out specifically what you want to do within a particular industry, you will be able to determine what type of elective classes to take.

The way most high schools and colleges are set up is that in order to take some elective classes, you have to have taken certain prerequisites. A prerequisite is simply a requirement that makes sure you take classes in the correct, sequential order. For example, you wouldn't take an "Advanced Biology" class before you take an "Introduction to Biology" class. The prerequisite to the "Advanced Biology" class is the "Introduction to Biology" class. Because of this, you will spend your first few semesters taking a lot of gen-ed classes because most of them are prerequisites for the elective classes you will want to take for your major.

Now, at this point, hopefully you're not stressing out too much about all this! I know some of it can seem overwhelming, but it really is fairly simple. The nice thing that colleges do when it comes to your classes is once you determine your major, they essentially direct you toward the classes you should take. One thing you should do is get a course catalog from any school that you are interested in. Schools will typically have a hard copy they can send you, but many will also have it available for download from their website. The course catalog will list every single class that school has to offer. It will also outline what the required classes are for each major. If you know what you want to major in, browse around at some different schools that are strong in that particular field, and find out what the requirements are for that major. That can help you to better determine what college may be a good fit for you.

chapter eight
what should I major in?

This is usually a difficult question, because if you're like most students, your answer today may be different than what you were interested in yesterday. Many of us have this form of "job A.D.D." where one day one type of profession seems appealing, but the next day, something completely different catches our attention. There may be several different majors that sound interesting, so it is difficult to know which is the best choice for you. As an example, Brown University in Rhode Island has more than 100 majors. The University of Iowa-Iowa City offers about 105, and undergrads at the University of Florida-Gainesville can choose from among 110 majors.

One of the primary reasons for choosing a major is to help create a more guided educational path towards your future career choice. But as we mentioned in the previous chapter, your first several semesters of college will probably be spent primarily on general education classes that are required, regardless of your major.

Because of this, there is nothing wrong with waiting a semester or two before you officially declare a major. You may plan to be an engineering major, but after taking a business class, you feel drawn towards business administration. When starting college, select classes in three or four areas that interest you. This allows you to test the waters to see if they're all you thought they would be. Until you nail down what you want to pursue, the best major for incoming students is "undecided." While this may sound strange, most schools will allow you to declare your major as "undecided" for at least a few semesters.

Choosing a major can certainly be difficult. One recommendation is to consider choosing a broader major as opposed to something extremely specific. That way you will have a wider scope of options in the future should you decide to change career paths, which you probably will at some point.

In fact, statistically, two out of three college students change their major at least once before graduation, and some may change it several times. Even if a student chooses one major and stays with that course of study for his entire college career, the average college graduate will still change jobs once every three years and completely change career fields two or three times in his lifetime![1] And quite honestly...that's all right! You shouldn't feel guilty about wanting to pull a one-eighty and go in a completely different direction with your college education. That is part of what college is for. It is the opportunity to learn more about yourself and who you are.

As you narrow it down and land on a degree choice, you have to ask yourself the question, what will I do with this degree? Remember that just because you graduate with a particular major doesn't necessarily mean that you have stay on that career path for the rest of your life. I'm a perfect example of that. I graduated in 2003 with a degree that now, just a few years later, I'm not directly utilizing. However, there was still plenty of valuable information I learned in college that I'm able to apply to my current career path. That is not necessarily a good thing or a bad thing, but it goes to show that a major doesn't lock you into a particular career path forever.

unusual college majors

If you're still unsure about what you're going to major in at college, consider these options from American colleges:

Ranch Management
Texas Christian University

Equestrian Business
Management
Stephens College

Dance Education
Birmingham-Southern College

Retail Floristry
Mississippi State University

Professional Nanny
Sullivan University

Adventure Recreation
Green Mountain College

Comedy: Writing & Performance
Humber College

Organic Agriculture
Washington State University

Although for a while you may wrestle with figuring out what you want that major to be, at some point you need to make a decision and dive in. Depending on your college, they may allow you to remain "undecided" for only a few semesters before you are required to declare your major. Remember that because different majors require different sets of classes, the longer you wait, the longer you may be putting off taking classes you need in order to graduate. And that may lengthen your overall college experience, which makes it more expensive. With this same principle in mind, some of the classes you took for your previous major may not be necessary with your new major, and can become unneeded (and expensive) credits. If you're unsure about this, it is always a good idea to check with your college counselor or advisor to make completely sure your existing credits will apply towards your new major.

Here's the bottom line: think through what you will major in but don't stress about it! While it is important, and you want to put some thought and effort into choosing your major, if you end up changing gears in the future, that's fine. It's not the end of the world. Find a major with classes that you absolutely love and go in that direction. Most students would rather sit in classes that they feel they are really getting something out of and learning from, than go through four years worth of classes that they can't stand.

You have to begin to realize that choosing a major is more than just choosing a particular career path. College is one of the first opportunities after high school that you have to truly prepare for the real world. You will not only learn from an educational standpoint, but you will also learn a lot about yourself. It is where you will learn more about yourself by finding out who you are, what you're passionate about, and further discovering what your likes and dislikes are.

College is the great bridge between **adolescence** and the **real world.**

chapter nine
what is college life like?

College life is that unique experience when, for the first time in your life, you experience the one thing you've been craving since the day you became a teenager. For the last 18 years or so, you've been living under the regime, rule and reign, dictatorship, loving home of Mom and Dad. But now your moment has arrived. You've served your time and now you're ready to have a moment like Mel Gibson in Braveheart. Scream it aloud with me: FREEDOM! That felt good, didn't it? (Hopefully you're not freaking out your roommate.)

For most students, college is their first taste of real freedom. Of living on your own. Of finding your place in this world. Of...well, you get the idea. We all know that freedom not only means different things to different people, but it also affects people in different ways! Some students think this new freedom comes with a license to act a little too crazy, which often leads to stupid decisions and poor judgment. Other students may have experienced more freedom in their upbringing and are mature enough to deal with it. Regardless, when you get to college, here's a simple principle to live by:

more freedom = more responsibility

We all want more freedom and more liberty to do the things we want, but we have to also remember that with additional freedoms come new responsibilities. At college, you won't have Mom or Dad there to tell you what to wear and what not to wear, whether or not you can have ice cream for breakfast, what time curfew is, or the people you shouldn't hang around. You're on your own now! And with that comes the responsibility of being an adult. That sounds weird doesn't it?!

However, once you become an adult, you have to start acting like one. Does that mean you shouldn't have fun? Does that mean you should be in bed by 8:30 every night? Does that mean you should live like a caveman and never come out of your room? Of course not!

College life is the great bridge between adolescence and the real world. You should have fun and enjoy every minute of it. Meet new people. Make new friends. Stay up late watching movies or playing video games. Go eat at a restaurant at 3:00 in the morning. Sing and dance in the rain (this is starting to sound like a musical). Have FUN! But just remember that you're an adult now, and that with the freedoms you now enjoy, comes the responsibility of making wise decisions.

And for goodness sake, call your mother every so often. She may cry herself to sleep if she doesn't hear from you every now and then. She gave birth to you. Raised you. Put up with all your randomness and craziness. Is a phone call too much to ask? (Sorry...your mom paid me to add that in!)

Learn from the freedoms and opportunities you have now. Prove to your parents and to others that you are a responsible and mature young adult, and that you will be able to handle the freedoms that college life offers you. When your parents give you a curfew, be respectful enough to be home by that time. If you tell someone you're going to do something, be mature enough to stick to your word. You'll be amazed that when you start acting like a responsible adult, people will start treating you like one.

chapter ten
should I get involved in extracurricular activities?

You may be one of the students that wants to get involved in anything and everything and truly experience all that college life has to offer. Or you may be that student who wants to sit back and check things out a little bit before you dive in to the buffet of options available to you.

From the day you arrive on campus, you're going to be bombarded with amazing opportunities. Think about all the different ways to get involved at a college: Greek life (fraternities and sororities), student government, intramural sports, and of course, the endless number of student clubs, groups, and organizations.

I recently came across a website for a major state university, and the main heading on the home page said this: "More Than 28,000 Potential Friends." Does anyone really need 28,000 friends?! Maybe on your Facebook page having 28,000 friends sounds kind of cool, but in college, are you kidding me? As I searched through this college's "Get Involved" section, I found over 500 different student organizations that you could join!

However good or bad it may be, that is the culture college life offers: an endless supply of potential friends and opportunities to fill your every waking moment. So how in the world do you even know where to begin? Let me give you a few ideas to consider:

go against the flow
All too often students join something just because It is popular. If the "cool" people are a part of a particular club or organization, then whether or not we want to admit it, we assume if we're part of that same group, we will also be considered "cool". This is what we call...STUPID! Regardless of who is part of a particular group or club, you need to find organizations and activities to be involved In that make sense for YOU!

stretch yourself
College is a great opportunity for you to explore, investigate, and discover who you are, what you like to do, and what you're good at. And often times the answers to these questions can be found by trying new things. Think about some of the things that you currently like to do or are good at. Before you tried that activity for the first time, you probably had some preconceived ideas of what it would be like. However, once you got into it, you may have found it to be completely different than what you expected. And apparently you really liked it or it was something you were really good at since you still do it today! Try something completely random, but keep an open mind in the process...you may like it!

do something, but not everything
Like I mentioned earlier, most colleges and universities have hundreds and hundreds of options to choose from when it comes to what there is to be involved with. While it is great to have a lot of options, it becomes difficult to know even where to begin. Think of it this way...

Have you ever been to a huge dinner buffet? I was speaking at an event recently, and for dinner one night, I went to this buffet that was inside the hotel where I was staying. Now when I say "buffet", we're talking this was the Mother of All Buffets! All other buffets would bow down to this buffet! It was that big! I felt like I hit the jackpot when I saw all the different types and varieties of food available. So I grabbed my first plate (first of many to come) and made my initial pass to get an overview of my options. The problem was that it all looked great, and I wanted to try a little bit of everything! But there was no way I could physically try everything that was available to me. I was struck with the "Paralysis of Analysis!" There were so many options and choices that it became overwhelming. I wanted to try everything, but I had no clue where to even begin!

The same idea applies to all the options you'll have at college. There are so many choices that it can become overwhelming. But if you go to a buffet and leave hungry, it's not the buffet's fault! You can't try everything on a buffet, and you can't join everything on campus. Pick out a few clubs, organizations, groups, or activities that you are really interested in and start there. If you don't like them or a group isn't what you expected it to be, just get a new plate and go back to the buffet!

While it's okay to spend some time with the "trial and error" method of finding organizations to be a part of, you don't want this pattern to become your entire college career! Whether you're in middle school, high school, or already in college, take time now to begin thinking about what things you are interested in doing. If you know what college you are planning to attend when you graduate, go ahead and get a guide for the various student organizations that are available. Get a list of a few clubs you might be interested in joining. Talk to people who are a part of that club. Ask questions. Figure out if it is a group worth trying out.

You certainly don't want to get to your senior year of college and look back with regrets over missed opportunities. At the same time, you don't want that to be the case as a middle school or high school student. Get involved today, and apply the same ideas listed above to where you are right now.

friends, family, & relationships:
can't live with them, can't live without them

how do I maintain friendships when we're miles apart?

We all have those friends in life who we're so close to that we can finish their sentences, we know what they are thinking, and we could tell stories about them that might even earn them prison time. Just a few hours or days in jail, so nothing that bad! But any time you move away from that person or any of your friends, things tend to change.

It's not that you want things to change or that you plan on them changing, but often times they just naturally do. When you live in the same city, and see each other every day, there is a natural bond and connection that forms from all that time spent together. But if you're 2,000 miles apart, that quality connection is difficult to maintain. It is certainly not impossible, but it is a challenge.

You've already figured out that as you get older, you learn more and more about who you are as a person. When that happens, it can naturally cause what you are looking for in a friend to evolve and change as well. As you look back over the years, you will probably notice that your friends in elementary school may be different than your friends in middle school. And your friends in middle school may be completely opposite from your friends in high school. It is not that one friend or group of friends was any better than any other group, but it is just the natural change that takes place. As you leave high school and enter the real world, that progression will just continue.

So how do you maintain your friendships when you move away? To start with, you really have to work at it. While nothing can replace quality time spent together, consistent and quality communication is a must. With the digital world that we live in, you can stay connected through email, blogs, social networking sites, instant messaging, and even video chatting. When I travel to speak at events, I always try to video chat with my wife and kids back home. Although I'm not physically there with them, it is amazing to be able to see that person live. Ah, the power of technology! But if you talk on the phone or email back and forth only once a month, then how valuable can your friendship really be? So your communication must be both quality and consistent.

As I think back to my friends from high school, there were some people who I was really close to that now I haven't spoken to in years. And others that I barely knew in high school are great friends of mine today. I say all of this not to discourage you that your friends will abandon you when you move away, but rather that you would realize that all friendships and relationships evolve and change, and that is okay.

chapter twelve
how will I make friends if I move away?

The first time you move away from home creates one of the most exhilarating and exciting feelings. However, as reality settles in, it can be one of the loneliest and scariest feelings. When you live in your home-town under a roof with your parents, it can become easy to take for granted how good you really have it. You probably have friends that live in your neighborhood and buddies that you've known since kindergarten (Don't you miss the nap times in kindergarten? Wow, that was random.). But once you move away, you feel like all of that will be left behind. And in a sense, that is true.

The reality is that after high school, when friends begin to move away for college or job opportunities, you will naturally drift apart from some friends, and there will be others you will stay very connected with. It is not that you mean to lose touch with someone or that you're mad at them, it's just that life has taken you in different directions. Like I said in the previous chapter, there is always some level of turnover with your friends. You will always be in a place in life where you will be making new friends. It isn't something that happens just when you graduate high school or move away. It is part of growing up and maturing in life. With that in mind, here are a few of things to consider when it comes to making friends:

friendships take time to develop

They don't happen overnight, so don't expect a "microwave" process. Think about your current friendships. None of them just happened. They took time. You have had your ups and downs and highs and lows, but those are the moments that solidify and strengthen your friendship. There is the old saying that "Rome wasn't built in a day." The same is true for friendships. For anything to have any lasting significance, it needs time to grow and develop.

making friends is risky business

Any time you try to start a friendship or relationship with another person, you are taking a risk. You are taking the chance that the other person may not like you, they may stab you in the back sometime in the future, or maybe they think you smell (do you?). You have to be willing to fully put yourself out there in a vulnerable position, although you may not get the same positive response back.

friendships don't just happen

You have to be proactive when it comes to making friends. I hate to burst your bubble, but when you move to a new area where you don't know anyone, people won't be lining up at your door to be your friend. It is not always like you see in the movies where people bring you baked cookies and cakes the day you move in! So if people aren't banging down your door to be your friend, that means the ball is in your court to go out and find them.

meet people where you live life

Odds are you're not going to find friends by browsing the personals, posting a message online or asking people at Wal-Mart to be your friend. You're more likely to find new friends in the places you already live life. If you're in college, you're likely to click well with people who are studying the same major as you. You can also meet people at the places you hang out (not Wal-Mart), where you work, and even get to know people in your dorm or apartment complex.

Even after I list all these possibilities for you, there are still some friendships that just happen completely randomly. One of your best friends is probably someone you disliked at one point, and another friend is someone who is a complete opposite from you. So when it comes to making new friendships, use the famous Nike slogan – get out there and "Just Do It!"

chapter thirteen

I miss my family...
is there something wrong with me?

There is absolutely nothing wrong with missing your family. You spent the first 18 years of your life with your family, so if you move out for college, it may be one of the first times you've been away from them for an extended period of time. Sure you went away to camp that one summer, and you cried yourself to sleep (you don't have to deny it...it's okay...I won't tell anyone) or all the nights you spent away at slumber parties. But to completely move away, where you may not see your family for several months, is a totally new challenge.

So when you're out on your own for the first time, it is completely normal to miss your family. Well, except for your younger brother. (Let's be honest. He was just a pain.) But it's okay to miss everyone else. Whenever you live on your own for the first time, it really is that feeling of leaving the nest and flying away. You're becoming an adult now (it sounds weird to hear that doesn't it?).

You have to allow yourself time to adjust to this new situation. Especially if you moved out of state or somewhere really far away (like Never, Never Land or Narnia), there is going to be a transition time for both you and your family. The first few weeks you may talk on the phone every day, but as the year goes on, you may only talk once a week. It isn't that you are growing apart or that you love your family any less, it is just the natural transition that begins to take place. My dad and I have a great relationship (he was the Best Man in my wedding), and we live about 10 minutes apart, but I may only see him a few times a month. We email and talk on the phone, but we may not see each other often. But that doesn't mean we're not close. It just means that we are both busy living life! The same thing may happen in your relationships. And that's okay.

When you move away, an interesting transition will take place in the relationship you have with your parents. Growing up, Mom and Dad are basically the bosses of the house. If they ask you to clean your room, it is usually not an optional request to complete only if it's convenient for you. But when you move out and are living on your own, your relationship with your parents will change. It isn't that you now have full rule and reign to disrespect them or never do anything they tell you. Think of it this way. As you grow into an adult, the role of a parent somewhat changes to that of a consultant. If I hire a consultant to help me with my business, his job is to provide feedback and advice, but it is my decision whether I will listen to that advice and apply it. Your mom and dad will be there to offer advice and counsel, but it is your responsibility to ask for it and determine if you will follow it.

If you've ever been in a serious dating relationship, then you know that the first few months are filled with goo-goo, ga-ga feelings and the belief that this other person can do no wrong. But the longer you're together, those feelings may begin to fade away and change. You still really like or love that person, but your relationship is evolving and maturing. The same will happen in your relationship with your family. Your relationships, not only with your parents, but with your siblings and your friends will change. Remember, it is not that you love each other any less, but rather it is just the natural evolution and progression of those relationships. And that's a good thing. You don't want to be Mommy's little baby-doll angel for the rest of your life...or do you?!

When you live on your own, you have an entirely new set of **freedoms** you didn't experience while living at home, but it also comes with a whole new set of **responsibilities.**

should I move back in with the fam?

When you're a teenager, you are literally counting down the days until you can move out of the house, and be on your own. You've probably already experienced some blow-up arguments with your parents where you "politely" reminded them of how soon you will be exiting the household. However you may discover that life on your own may not be all it is cracked up to be.

Don't get me wrong. Living on your own is exciting. You have an entirely new set of freedoms you didn't experience while living at home, but it also comes with a whole new set of responsibilities. Because of that, you may begin to have some feelings of being home sick. Like I mentioned in a previous chapter, missing your family is normal (except for your annoying little brother). There is nothing at all wrong with missing your family and even admitting that part of you would like to move back home. But determining whether you're just mildly home sick or if you should really move home can be a big decision.

If your parents are cool with it, I would highly recommend living at home for a few semesters while you're in college. You will save a ridiculous amount of money compared to paying for room and board at a dorm. The problem with living on campus is that it can be crazy expensive. When I was in college, I lived in the dorms for a year and then moved back home to save money. I enjoyed dorm life, and my roommate was one of my best friends, but that doesn't change how pricey it is to live in the dorm.

Another factor to consider is how responsible and mature you are. Let's be honest...some students just aren't ready to live on their own. Some are irresponsible and would be a disaster by themselves! Although Mom and Dad don't need to hold your hand and change your diapers when you're 21 years old, sometimes just the added accountability of living at home is beneficial.

You need to remember, though, that if you are living at home, it doesn't matter how old you are, you are living under your parents' roof, and you need to play by their rules. If they give you a curfew, you need to be respectful enough to be home by that curfew regardless of how old you are. If they ask for your help with the laundry or mowing the grass, consider it part of your rent for getting to live there. If you're going to gripe about their rules all the time, then get a place of your own, and you may quickly realize how good you had it.

If you decide to move back home, understand there is nothing to be ashamed of, and there is certainly nothing wrong with living with your parents. You need to also remember that you can't live with Mommy and Daddy forever. As much as they love you, and as much as they may deny it, they are really looking forward to having the house back to themselves! I know it's comfortable and cozy in your bedroom with your Scooby Doo bed sheets and your Mickey Mouse night light, but at some point, you just have to grow up and move out on your own! Spread your wings and fly, young grasshopper (man, that was corny).

chapter fifteen
how do I break up with someone?

Cue the music: *Breaking up is hard to do!* Sorry, I couldn't help myself, but never have truer words been sung! Breaking up really is hard to do. That is unless you woke up one morning and realized you hated his guts or if something happened in your relationship that could land you on Jerry Springer. Then, breaking up is easy!

But if you're in a relationship, that just isn't working, and you don't see much potential, ending it can be extremely difficult for many reasons. You never want to hurt someone else. You don't want to let other people down. Your CDs are still in his truck! There are numerous reasons that make breaking up a difficult thing. But if you reach the conclusion that you should break up, here are some steps to follow:

make a decision
There's nothing worse than being in a relationship that you know you shouldn't be in, but not having the guts to make a decision about it. We know you don't want to hurt him, and we know it's going to be tough (didn't we already establish that breaking up is hard to do?), but at some point you've got to make a decision to either make it work or move on. If you decide that you need

to break up, set yourself a deadline (no more than a week) to have "the talk" and stick to it. If you're in a relationship and are consistently miserable, then is it really smart to linger around hoping maybe someday things will improve?

have the talk

Ahh, the talk...the dreaded talk! Let's be honest: no one wants to be on the giving or receiving end of this conversation. And we've all heard the classic break up lines. "It's not you, it's me." "I just want to be friends." "I want to see other people." And finally, "I'm sorry; I thought you were someone else." Ouch! That never feels good any way you look at it. But if you're going to have "the talk," one of the biggest things you owe yourself and the other person is honesty. While you want to be sensitive to his feelings (especially if this is blind-siding him), you need to be straight-up about how you feel. You both deserve honesty from each other.

world's worst break up lines

Here are some of the world's worst break-up lines. Please don't use these. You can come up with something better:

Sorry, my doctor said I have to cut out all fat.

Well, what am I saying...I don't even want to be FRIENDS anymore.

It was between you and my imaginary friend Bobo...Sorry.

I've discovered my inner child and we've decided that you're icky.

Better luck next time.

I just can't love someone who would love someone like me.

It's not me; it's you.

My dog is concerned I'm not spending enough time with him.

move on

After you've had "the talk," you've cried all you can cry, and you have had enough snot bubbles pouring out of your nose, then comes the process of picking up the pieces and moving on. There are several elements to think about that can help with this. After a break-up, it is easy to fall into a depression and think the world is coming to an end. But life goes on, and the world isn't going to self destruct, so you shouldn't either. You don't need to be looking for the next relationship, so slow down and take the time for you to be you. Spend time with friends and family, and let some of those wounds you may be feeling begin to heal. As for your relationship with that other person, it is certainly possible for you two to remain friends. But at least for the following few months, it would be smart to have a little space. You're both hurting, and continuing to spend time together after a break up just further complicates the situation.

I feel like I'm a broken record: *Breaking up is hard to do!* But it's part of life and is part of what helps shape and form who you are as a young adult. Once you've made that decision, stick to it. You don't need to be persuaded out of it by that other person. You have to determine what is best for you. Have that dreaded talk and then begin the process of moving on. And if you're on the receiving end of "the talk," continue reading.

chapter sixteen

I just got dumped...now what?

Let me first say, if the person who just broke up with you did so because of the previous chapter, then forgive me and don't be bitter as you read the rest of this book! But at one point or another, we've all been dumped, and let's just be honest... it is a pretty crappy feeling. No one wants to feel rejected, unloved, unwanted, abandoned (I'm getting bummed out just writing this sentence!), or any other adjective to describe what you may be feeling.

I know it's frustrating and confusing, and you have a wide range of emotions running through your head. You wonder what other people will think, or how your "status" will be affected (it won't, by the way). You wonder if there is someone else this person is interested in, or if there was anything you could have done differently to change the situation. Being the "dumpee" (I just made that word up) is no fun but the reality is that getting dumped is just part of the relationship experience. So where do you go from here? How do you begin to pick up the pieces and move on? Here are a few thoughts that may help:

let it out
Any time we experience something difficult like a break-up, it is easy to bottle up all of those emotions and feelings. We

become this hermit crab; we want to sleep all day, we don't want to see anyone, and if we're not careful, it becomes easy to slip into a depression. A very simple principle to remember is this: if you don't let it out, it stays bottled up inside. You may be thinking, "Thanks for stating the obvious there, Einstein!" But it's true that if you don't let those feelings and emotions out, they began to hurt you from within. It's okay to cry. It's okay to be sad. It's okay to be frustrated and confused. But you have to let those emotions out. Spend time with the friends and family who love and care for you and just vent for a while. You're basically emotionally throwing up on them! Grab the Kleenex box and go let it out.

be mature about it

Being on the short end of a break-up can cause people to do some strange things! We want to try to show that person how much she means to us or how important this relationship is, and when that happens, sometimes we don't always use the best judgment. When you're hurting, it can become easy to make decisions that you will later regret. Don't stalk her, don't harass her, don't spread rumors about her, or gossip to anyone who will listen. Rather, be mature and begin picking up the pieces to move on.

there are other fish in the sea

This is such a cliché, and I debated whether to even put it on the list, but regardless of how corny it may sound, it is true. You may be thinking, "I know there are other fish in the sea, but I liked the fish I had!" That may be the case, but remember this: you have no idea what the future holds, so is it possible that you were settling for someone good when the future may bring you someone great? I know you may be feeling discouraged, confused and frustrated, but haven't you found that all things happen for a reason? It may not make any sense now, but you may be able to look back in a few months or years, and it will all be clearer at that point.

I know it is difficult any time you feel hurt or rejected by another person. But that is part of the risk-reward side of relationships. You put yourself out there and try to make a connection with someone, and sometimes he feels the same connection. But sometimes, for whatever reason, he doesn't. That doesn't mean you are a bad person or there is anything wrong with you. It just means that it is his loss! So hang in there, and remember tomorrow is a new day.

chapter seventeen
how do I balance a relationship with the rest of my schedule?

Adding a relationship to your already busy schedule can be a delicate dance. When you add a new relationship to the mix, you are now being pulled in one more direction that you weren't before, and depending on how much you like this other person, this new relationship may become a major priority for you rather quickly. There must be a balance, because although you want to spend as much time as possible with this person, you still have to go to work, keep your grades up, and hopefully have time to take a shower (otherwise that relationship may be over sooner than you think!). So in order to successfully balance a relationship, here are some things to remember:

set boundaries
You have to set boundaries for yourself. If you don't determine how you will best utilize your time, someone or something else will determine it for you. You may want to set boundaries regarding how late you'll be out on a particular night or how many nights a week you'll be gone. It may seem childish at first, but remember that when you're out on your own, Mommy and Daddy aren't there to make sure you get enough sleep and take care of yourself. With this new freedom comes the responsibility to act like an adult.

don't isolate yourself

A major mistake that many new couples make is to isolate themselves from the rest of the world. If you really like someone, of course you want to be with her as much as possible, but don't forget the other people in your life. If you begin blowing off family members and friends to be with the new love interest in your life, that is not going to set well with other people. You don't want to be dissed by one of your friends just because they have a new relationship, so don't do that to others.

'you' comes before 'us'

You may be absolutely head-over-heels for the new dude or dudette in your life, and it can become easy to be so engrossed in being a part of this new couple that you forget to take the time for you. Who you are as an individual is more important than your status as a couple. If you, as an individual, aren't a whole, healthy person, what makes you think that you're going to have a strong relationship? If you end up trying to find your identity in this other person or this relationship, you will always be miserable. Sorry to disappoint you. Take time for 'you' before you take time for 'us'.

One of the best things you can do is determine *now* how you will handle a relationship if one should begin to develop. We all know that when you're infatuated with puppy love, the only thing that matters is being with that other person. The rest of world can just get lost for all you care! To prevent becoming that kind of person when you're in a relationship, take time now to evaluate how important a new relationship will be. And if you're already in a serious relationship, step back and think through these points to make sure you have a healthy balance between your relationship and the rest of your life.

chapter eighteen

SEX: if I love someone, why not?

Ok, let's be honest for a second. You started flipping through the table of contents just a second ago, saw those three big letters staring back at you, and you immediately came to this chapter! Maybe this should be the introduction chapter, since all teenagers want to read about this first anyway! So since you're here, let's go ahead and talk about that big, scary word... SEX.

Often times, students think, "If I love someone, why shouldn't we have sex? It is our way to express our love for one another." (Either that, or you are both in heat!) But the truth is that having premarital sex can cause much more long term pain than it's worth. I understand there is a lot of pressure to have sex, and sometimes it is just the sheer curiosity to know what it is like. But whenever you're involved with premarital sex, you're trading a moment of pleasure for a potential lifetime of pain. To me, it's not worth the risk. Here are some risks with premarital sex:

diseases
Let me just cut to the chase with the facts: Researchers at the Federal Center for Disease Control and Prevention found at least one in four teenage American girls has a sexually transmitted

disease. Among those who admitted having sex, the rate was even higher – 40% had an STD.[1] Think about that for a second. If you're sexually active, that means you may have as high as a 40% chance of already having an STD. Your odds aren't much better than a coin toss. In addition, each year three million teens are infected with STD's, and two-thirds of all new STD infections occur among young people under age 25.[2]

pregnancy
Chances are you know of a teenage girl at your school or in your community who is pregnant or had a baby while in school. As I travel around the country speaking in high school assemblies, I'm amazed at the number of girls I meet who are pregnant. Statistics tell us that of the approximately 750,000 teen pregnancies that occur each year, 82% are unintended. On top of that, more than one-quarter of those end in abortion.[3] No girl thinks that she will get pregnant, and no guy thinks he will get a girl pregnant.

emotional baggage
STDs and pregnancy are outcomes that you can measure, but the emotional baggage that lies beneath the surface can be much more difficult to identify. You can't measure guilt, regret, lowered self-esteem, and the emotional scars that are left behind from premarital sex. But realize those things are as real as pregnancy and disease. One study of youth in grades 7-11 found that engaging in premarital sex often leads to depression. In addition, they are more likely to commit suicide.[4] Plus, the fact that premarital sex is also likely to lead to promiscuity and future divorce.

Maybe you've heard some of these stats and facts before, or maybe it is brand new information to you. But the fact is that you don't think about these things in the heat of the moment. If you think it couldn't happen to you, or that these statistics don't apply to your world, you're kidding yourself. Instead of being naïve and assuming you'll be fine, you would be wise to think these things through now before you're in a situation where you may not use your best judgment. Although I don't know of any formal study on the subject, my guess would be that if you asked teenagers who had experienced a teen pregnancy, contracted an STD, or carried around emotional scars from a sexual relationship, nearly 100% thought it wouldn't happen to them. We all think we're immune until the statistic becomes a reality.

If you're in a relationship, remember that you should never be pressured into doing anything you're not comfortable with. That doesn't make you a prude. That doesn't make you less popular. It just means that you have a backbone and are willing to stand up for something you believe in. If you're in a relationship, and the other person is pressuring you to do something that you don't want to do, that is not a relationship you need to be in. Some people can be extremely controlling and manipulative in a relationship, and that's not healthy for either of you.

Let me make a disclaimer here to wrap up this chapter. Waiting to have sex until you are married is extremely difficult. You have all of these emotions and hormones raging through your body, and you feel like this caged animal just waiting for your moment to break free! I know, I know, I get it. The ideas we've discussed throughout this chapter will serve you well in many other areas of life. You have got to learn how to delay gratification. Society pushes you to experience instant gratification, but waiting to have sex until you're married is worth the wait. I know because I did. My wife and I dated for five years, and we didn't have sex until we were married. Was it easy? Heck no! She's really hot! But was it worth it to wait? Absolutely.

this relationship is getting serious...
what do I do?

It was just yesterday when you saw him in the hall and thought he was kind of cute. Then through your network of friends, rumors were swirling that he kind of liked you, and that he might even ask you out. A few days later that moment arrived.

Your eyes met through the sea of students and then, as if completely unscripted, "Endless Love" started playing over the intercom speakers (strange, I know). You took it as a sign, and started walking towards him. You made some small talk, and then it happened. He asked you out on a date. Sure it was just to McDonald's, and his mom had to drive you there, but you were together. At least that's what you told yourself.

That first date was such a rush of emotion, wasn't it? You found out you liked each other, you had a lot in common, and somehow during that first date, you found yourself talking about how much you liked his hair. For the first few weeks of this new relationship, it all seemed like this fairy tale, made-for-Disney story. You talked on the phone all the time. You spent every waking moment together. And before long, what began as this flirty, fun little relationship starts evolving into something you hadn't expected it to become. It started getting...serious...(cue scary music) dum, dum, dum. So what do you do now?

As a relationship begins to get more and more serious, often times there is a sense of nervousness and anxiety that starts to set in. That is natural, so don't be alarmed. But at the same time, there's a reason that brain of yours is setting off signal flares to get your attention. When that relationship starts getting a little more serious, here are some things to consider:

don't panic

It's funny how sometimes we start getting really nervous when a relationship starts becoming serious. But let me ask you: what did you think was going to happen?! When a couple has been together for a significant period of time, it is just natural that long-term thinking begins to enter the equation. Thoughts start racing through your mind that maybe, just maybe, this is "The One." Perhaps you have stumbled upon that one, true soul mate that was destined for you, and he just happened to be in your fourth-period math class. Anytime you have these thoughts flooding into your mind, it can cause you to panic! But remain calm. When you start panicking, it can lead to poor judgment and stupid decisions.

slow down

When is comes to a relationship, here's a simple principle to live by: it is better to go slow and get it right, than to speed it up and get it wrong. As a relationship gets more and more serious, it can start as this small, innocent snowball that begins rolling down the hill. But next thing you know, it has turned into an avalanche of destruction that is impossible to stop. The best thing you can do with a relationship that is starting to get serious is to slow down. Regardless of what you may think, time only helps strengthen relationships. When you slow down and remind yourself that there is no rush, you make better decisions and avoid moments of stupidity. My wife and I started dating in high school and got married on our five year anniversary. Five years we dated! And you know what? I wouldn't change a thing about it. That extra time allowed us to not only get to know each other better, but also to allow our relationship to develop on a solid foundation.

ask the tough questions

When you've been together with someone for a while and things begin to get serious, it is time to start asking the tough questions. What brought you two together in tho first place (attraction) will not be enough to sustain a relationship for the long haul. Enjoy that gorgeous hair he has now, because someday it's going to fall out! You have to take the time to ask the difficult questions about your individual goals, dreams, future plans, attitudes, integrity, etc. What does that other person plan on doing with the next five years of his life? How does that compare with what you want to do in that time? What does he want to be when he grows up? Is he "growing up" now, or his he still young and immature? Do you enjoy being with him, or do you constantly bicker and fight? Is this someone you want to spend your life with, or is this just a fun, cute relationship that has no potential for the future? Ask the difficult questions to evaluate not only where you are, but also where you see this going.

get feedback

When you're in a serious relationship, it can be very easy for your judgment to become clouded. It is like having "love glasses" on that fog your vision to what your relationship and that person may really be like. You may feel like it is you two against the world, but you would be ignorant to ignore the opinions and advice of others. While you may tend to see only the good in someone, the rest of your family and friends may think you're blind to what a loser he is! Be honest with others, and get feedback from your parents, trusted friends, and people whose opinions you value and respect. It may confirm that the relationship is a good thing, but on the other hand, they may see red flags in the other person or the relationship that you have missed. Not only should you ask for feedback, but be open-minded enough to listen and take it seriously.

After asking the difficult questions and getting some honest feedback from others, what happens if you find yourself thinking that maybe this isn't the right relationship for you? You need to make a decision and move on. But how exactly do you do that? Flip back to chapter 15 for some help!

when will I be ready for marriage?

Any time you've been dating someone for a fair amount of time, the subject of marriage inevitably comes up. Sometimes your friends begin asking the questions about how serious the relationship is. Of course your mom wants to know what's going on! Or maybe your girlfriend just comes right out and asks when she will be getting a ring! That's a scary and exciting feeling when you get to a point in a relationship where you are beginning to consider this person as marriage material. How do you know if you, personally and together as a couple, are ready for marriage? Consider these questions:

are you on the same page?
Author Dave Ramsey, says that before you get married, you should be in agreement on four big areas: money, religion, in-laws, and kids. Think about it. These are some of the biggest, hot-button issues in relationships. As it relates to money, are you a spender or a saver? What if you have completely different religious views and beliefs? What if your significant other wants to live next door to her parents? If you want one kid, and she believes that kids are cheaper by the dozen, then you're going to have issues! If you haven't addressed these subjects with the person you're dating, then you're not ready for marriage.

is it the right time?

The right thing at the wrong time is still the wrong thing. It happens all too often that boy meets girl, they go on a couple of dates, and then start planning to be married within a few months. I don't think that is smart at all. So when is the right time? While every couple and every situation is different, I think you should date at least one year before you get engaged or consider getting married. My wife and I dated for five years, although some of that was while we were in high school. But the more time you have with someone, the more you get to know her beyond the initial infatuation stage of a relationship. If it takes a baby nine months to develop and grow, it should take a relationship at least that long!

are you ready?

Let me go ahead and state the obvious: marriage is a lifelong commitment. Unfortunately in our culture, many people view marriage as this: "If it doesn't work out, it's no big deal, we'll just get a divorce." But nobody goes into a marriage planning to get a divorce. At least not normal, sane people! Marriage changes everything about your priorities. No longer is it about you. There is now this other person that you must be willing to die for. Whenever you get married, the minister reminds you this is for better or worse, sickness and in health, and richer or poorer...or really, really poorer (that's what the first few years of marriage are like!). Marriage doesn't work only when it is convenient for you. Because it is such a major commitment, you have to evaluate: Are you ready?

If you've been in a relationship for a long period of time and you don't plan on getting married, then I have to ask the question, what's the point? Part of the purpose of dating is so you can determine if this is someone that you want to spend the rest of your life with. If it's not, then you should be honest and caring enough for yourself and the other person to move on from the relationship. There is no sense in misleading someone or giving her the wrong impression about how you see the future of the relationship. Guys, don't lead girls on. That's not cool. And girls, the same goes for you. Don't play around with a guy's feelings. We're fragile.

finances:
show me the money

chapter twenty-one
so many things, so little money!

Unfortunately, managing money is one subject that students may need the most help with in life, but get the least amount of training. I can't stress to you enough how important it is to take steps now, regardless of your age or where you're at in life, to learn how to handle money. Money (or the lack of it) can become one of the biggest stresses in life if you're not careful. So let's jump into this and look at six things you have to do if you're going to learn how to manage your money:

create a game plan

In order to win with money, you have to know how much you have coming in and how much you have going out. You need to know where your money is going, so it doesn't just walk out of your wallet, as it may be doing now. In order to do all of this and effectively manage your money, you need a game plan. This is more commonly known as the dreaded "B" word. Not *that* "B" word, you filthy animal. Get your head out of the gutter. I'm talking about making a budget (cue scary music, screams, lightning, thunder, etc.). I'm going to talk more about the specifics of making a budget in the next chapter, but the idea is this...you have to have one! A budget is essentially a road map for handling your money. If you were going on a road trip, you would take the time to map out on Google or Map Quest where you were going and how you needed to get there. A budget is the same thing for your money. You have to have a game plan, otherwise you'll always end up with more month than money (figure that out!).

plan for rainy days

You have to plan for emergencies, because they *will* happen. It is not a matter of if it is going to rain, but rather when it does rain, do you have an umbrella? In case you haven't noticed, life happens. That's just the way it goes. So if you know it is going to rain, and you are going to have emergencies pop up in your life, wouldn't it just be smart to plan for them? If you plan for life's surprises, then it's no longer a big emergency, is it? Now it is more of an inconvenience, which is a pain, but it isn't that big of a deal. Think of the rainy days that happen in life: your transmission goes out on your car, your college textbooks get stolen, you end up in the hospital for a few days, or your apartment blows up (that's really bad). Those are the things that you think will never happen to you and yet when they do, you're up a creek.

For most students, I would recommend having a rainy day/ emergency fund of $500 but preferably $1,000. For some of you, that may seem like a million dollars, and for others, you may think that is no big deal. But having $500 in the bank will catch the majority of emergencies that will come up in your world. This money should be put in a savings account, and should never be used unless it is an emergency. Spring Break in Cancun is not an emergency. Christmas is not an emergency. It is always on the same day in December. They don't move it. If you know it is coming, you should plan for it.

avoid debt like the plague

I'm talking about all kinds of debt...credit card debt, school loans, car loans, any type of debt...avoid it at all costs. Unfortunately, most Americans accept debt as a way of life. They say, "I'm always going to have a car payment." Or "I'm always going to have a credit card balance." That's stupid. If you can't pay cash for it, wait and save up until you can. Again, it goes back to that idea of delayed gratification. There's no sense in going into debt for some electronic gadget, a new outfit, or to go to the movies. Pay cash or don't get it. If you currently have debt, the only way you're ever going to get out of debt is to stop borrowing money. Think if you were stuck in a hole. As you tried to get out, you continued to dig down a few more feet, and make the hole just a little bigger. That's ridiculous. Quit borrowing money!

save like crazy
We are going to talk about this in the chapter about savings, but you will quickly learn the power of compound interest. Wouldn't it be great if you started saving now, so you could be stinking rich when you're 40? What if you were so loaded that you could visit a store in the mall and just buy the entire store? Or maybe even the entire mall. That would be fun, wouldn't it? But again, that means delaying gratification now, so you can win later.

think long term
Do you remember the story about the tortoise and the hare? More importantly, do you remember who came out on top? The way I remember it, the tortoise always wins the race. If you learn to make sacrifices today, it will always pay off in the long term. Personal finance is 80% behavior and 20% head knowledge. I can give you the knowledge you need, but it really comes down to changing your behaviors and applying the things you read in this book to life in the real world.

give it away
It may sound strange, but one of the best things you can do with money is give it away. Weird, I know. But think about a time when you gave someone a gift, and you knew it really meant a lot to them. You put so much effort and thought into the present that to see their reaction was worth it all. At the risk of sounding like a Hallmark card, you really can't put a price

on that feeling. When you've been smart with your money, you then have the ability, the opportunity, and maybe even the responsibility to help others.

I know, I know. You're thinking all of these ideas look great on paper, but in real life, they are pretty difficult to carry out. But the fact is that managing your money isn't that difficult, even though many people are convinced they can't do it. So they come up with excuses about money management, when really they are just lazy! You can do each and every one of these things listed. Is it easy? Not necessarily. Is it worth it? Absolutely!

I can say this because I've been on both sides of the coin. Coming out of college, my wife and I had nearly $25,000 in debt. Car debt, credit cards, school loans...you name it, we had it. But we have followed these principles for handling and managing our money and today, we are debt-free except for our house. No more credit card debt. No car payments. No school bills. And do you know how that feels? To say it feels "really good" is a massive understatement. Instead of sending our money to all of these other people in the form of payments, now we get to keep it for ourselves, and do with it as we please. That is a great feeling of freedom, both personally and financially.

chapter twenty-two
how do I make a budget?

So we're back to that dreaded "B" word again, aren't we? Like I mentioned in the previous chapter, a budget is a necessary evil if you are going to win with money. But for most of us, we think we can live without that budget. We assume we won't stick to it, so what's the point of making one in the first place? We assume it never works the way we wrote it out. We figure that if we're not good with numbers or that we have to use our fingers and toes for counting, then we'll be a disaster at putting together a budget. But creating a budget and sticking to it can be done and done well. Here are a few principles for making a budget:

make a new budget every month
Sometimes we think we can make this error-free budget from heaven that will work on any given month. But I think we're all smart enough to realize there is no such thing as a perfect month. Your income and expenses will almost always vary, and that is something you have to plan for. At the end of every month, my wife and I sit down and make a new budget. Every month is different, and you ought to plan accordingly.

write it down

A lot of us like to think we have our budget in our head. It's stuck up there, and we can remember it perfectly. But that just doesn't work! You have to write it down. Part of the reason you're doing this is to create a visual goal for yourself. According to Brian Tracy, a motivational speaker, a recent study of Harvard graduates found that after two years, the three percent who had written down their goals achieved more financially than the other 97 percent combined!

use the envelope system

The envelope system is a process in which you pay for as much stuff as possible in cash. Here's how it works. The first thing you do is determine the common expenses that you can pay for in cash. These are categories such as groceries, gas, entertainment, clothing, eating-out, etc. Once you have set up your budget, and you know what the amounts are for each of these categories, go through and withdraw the budgeted amount in cash from your checking account and stick each amount in its own envelope. This is a way to force yourself to budget. When you need to buy groceries, you take money from the grocery envelope and spend only that. Any change left over goes back into the grocery envelope. If you only have $20 left in grocery envelope, and it's only the seventh of the month, you're going to be eating a lot of Ramen noodles!

Think about why this works so well. Let's say you go to the mall and pay for your purchases with a debit card. You've made a budget, and you know you have $50 to spend so you've picked out $50 worth of stuff to buy. But as you're walking up to pay for it, you notice a great shirt that's on sale for only $10. Ten bucks! No big deal, so you go ahead and add it to the pile, and your total comes to around $60. You know you're $10 over, but what's the big deal? But what if you used the envelope system and paid for your items in cash...guess what? If you walk into the mall with just a $50 bill, you're not leaving with $60 worth of stuff unless you want to be arrested!

My wife and I have used this system for almost two years now, and I'll tell you...it works! You are forced to pay attention to where your money is going, and how you are spending it. On top of that, when you pay for something in cash, it is more difficult than just swiping a card. If I go the grocery store, and my tab is $100, it is much more difficult to hand the cashier a crisp $100 bill, as opposed to just swiping a piece of plastic that I don't have to think about. At least try the envelope system for a couple of months, and if you don't like it, then you can go back to your system: being broke!

spend every dollar before the month begins

You want to create a zero-based budget. In one month, you figure every dollar of income you have coming in and every dollar of expenses going out. Then you do the math to make a zero come out at the bottom. Your income minus your expenses should equal zero for that month. When you pay attention to where your money is going, you will be shocked at how much you spend in some areas, and how little you spend in others. But you don't know unless you write it down and have a plan.

Let me reiterate. If you want to win with money, you've got to make a budget. Every month. Accounting for every dollar. You have to do it. The first couple of times you make a budget, it may be a complete disaster. You may even prefer to have a root canal instead. But I promise you, if you work at it and stick to it, each month you make a budget will be a little easier than the previous. Before long, you'll be able to do a budget in your sleep. And when *that* happens, you're on your way to being wealthy well into the future! When that happens, remember you're supposed to give money away (to me for example...you read the last chapter didn't you?).

chapter twenty-three
do I need a banking account?

At some point, keeping your money in a piggy bank is no longer going to work! You're going to want to look for some new options. This means you probably need to open an account at a bank. You may have several questions about having a banking account, so let's try to answer some of them.

how do I choose a bank?

Depending on where you live, there are probably a crazy number of options when it comes to selecting a bank. Your choices range from major, national banks (i.e. Bank of America or Wells Fargo) to locally owned banks to credit unions. You have a lot of choices and, at times, it may seem overwhelming. For the most part, banks all do the same thing. They keep your money safe until you need it. But here are some additional items to consider when choosing a bank:

location

Think about what banks are close to your home, your job, and the other places you live life. Consider not only proximity to where you live but also consider the number of locations a bank may have in your area. If you decide to go with a nationally-known bank, chances are there are several locations, not just in your area, but around the country as well. This is nice from a convenience standpoint, but the trade off is that the bigger the bank, the less personal service you may receive. At the same time, you may get better customer service with a local bank, but if they only have one location in your city, it may not be as convenient for you.

fees

Make sure you are clear about what, if any, fees a bank may charge for having an account with them. You can find numerous banks today that offer free accounts, so I would recommend talking with one of them. Also, some banks say they have "free" accounts, but may have certain conditions. For example, they may be free as long as you maintain a certain balance in your account or if you make a certain number of purchases using your debit card each month.

account features

In addition to location and fees, there are some additional things you may consider when picking a bank. For example, do you need any type of online bill paying service? I get this service free from my bank, and it is one of the reasons I have my accounts with them. Another regular feature I use is online banking. I can log into the bank's website and view transactions made within my account. Some banks offer free checks when you open a new account, so that may be something to consider.

how do I open a banking account?

Once you figure out where you would like to bank at, opening an account is a pretty simple process. You will need to go to one of the local bank branches and ask for someone that can help you open an account. If you are under 18, most banks will probably require one of your parent's signature, so keep that in mind as well. Don't forget to bring some money with you so you can make your initial deposit into the account. You will sign a few papers, they will give you some temporary checks (they will send your other checks in the mail), and you should be good to go.

what type of account do I need to open?

The type of account you want to open will depend on what you will use it for. If you are setting aside money for something specific such as a car or college expenses, it is better to open a savings account. But if you plan on using the money in that account on a regular basis, then you will probably want to open a checking account. It may not be a bad idea to have both a checking and a savings account.

In today's culture, it is very difficult to live without a banking account of some kind. And if you ever don't like the bank you're using, you can always withdraw all the money in your account and move it to a different bank. Just make sure you are paying attention to your money and are keeping it in something other than a piggy bank!

should I be saving money for retirement?

You don't need to stress about retirement right now, but it is a smart idea to begin thinking about it. It sounds overly simple, but if you begin preparing for the future now, you can retire as a very wealthy person! In fact, you will have a major advantage over your parents in planning for retirement, because you have one key element on your side:

time

In order to best utilize the time that is on your side, you have to apply one principle we've talked about throughout the book: delayed gratification. Instead of spending $20 now, wait several years, make smart decisions along the way, and it could be worth $200. However, given the choice between $20 now or $200 in several years, most students would probably take the cash now. Planning for retirement is about making smart decisions and being disciplined now, so you can win long term. In order to utilize the time that is on your side, you have to understand a powerful principle that would make your math teacher very proud.

compound interest

Maybe you've heard of compound interest before, or maybe you skipped that day of school, but either way, it's a pretty simple concept. It is the idea of adding accumulated interest back to the original principal amount, so that you are earning interest on top of your interest. It's pretty cool when you think about it. Let me give you an example. Let's say I'm going to give you some money (I knew I liked this guy), but I'm going to let you select how you want me to give it to you. Here are your two choices:

1. Ten thousand dollars every day for 30 days.
2. One penny that doubles every day for 30 days.

Now most people would probably take the ten thousand dollars per day right? Think about it...that's $300,000! That's tough to turn down. But let's do the math and figure out which is the better option.

	Option #1	Option #2
Day 1	$10,000.00	$.01
Day 2	$20,000.00	$.02
Day 3	$30,000.00	$.04
Day 4	$40,000.00	$.08
Day 5	$50,000.00	$.16
Day 6	$60,000.00	$.32
Day 7	$70,000.00	$.64 (this is my weekly allowance)
Day 8	$80,000.00	$1.28
Day 9	$90,000.00	$2.56
Day 10	$100,000.00	$5.12
Day 11	$110,000.00	$10.24
Day 12	$120,000.00	$20.48
Day 13	$130,000.00	$40.96
Day 14	$140,000.00	$81.92
Day 15	$150,000.00	$163.84 (I need a calculator)
Day 16	$160,000.00	$327.68
Day 17	$170,000.00	$655.36
Day 18	$180,000.00	$1,310.72

Day 19	$190,000.00	$2,621.44
Day 20	$200,000.00	$5,242.88
Day 21	$210,000.00	$10,485.76 (my head hurts)
Day 22	$220,000.00	$20,971.52
Day 23	$230,000.00	$41,943.04
Day 24	$240,000.00	$83,886.08
Day 25	$250,000.00	$167,772.16
Day 26	$260,000.00	$335,544.32 (bye, bye option #1)
Day 27	$270,000.00	$671,088.64
Day 28	$280,000.00	$1,342,177.28 (I need another comma)
Day 29	$290,000.00	$2,684,354.56
Day 30	$300,000.00	$5,368,709.12

Not much of a contest, huh? You probably wish you had picked that penny option! This is a great example of how quickly money can multiply, but now let's look at it from a practical standpoint.

Let's say on your 18th birthday, you put $1,000 in a savings account, and you never deposit or withdraw anything from that account until age 65 when you retire. That's 47 years. Remember, just a one-time $1,000 investment that you never touch.

• At 6% interest per year (a nice savings bond), you will have just over $16,000 at age 65. Not bad for a $1,000 investment.

• At 12% interest per year (solid mutual funds), your total amount will double to around $32,000, right? But in fact, you will have over $230,000!

• At 18% interest per year (real estate), that initial $1,000 deposit will end up making you a multi-millionaire. You will have about $2.8 million at age 65!

Now while each of these interest rates are realistic, the higher the interest rate, the greater the risk. You can get a 6% return on a savings bond with little to no risk, but getting 18% on a piece of real estate is going to be extremely risky. There are certainly pros and cons either way, and while the interest rates aren't necessarily the issue, I want you to understand the power of starting early.

Remember slow and steady wins the race. Here's one more example. Suppose you started at age 18 and saved for 47 years until age 65, saving only $50 per month at a 12% average annual return. Although you would have saved only around $29,000, at the end of 47 years you would have nearly $1.3 million, thanks to all the interest you earned.

Not to over-simplify it, but if you start now and are consistent in putting away money for retirement, you will be loaded with cash sooner than you think! But it takes delaying gratification today, so that you can win tomorrow.

Again, it is important to determine what you want to do with the money in order to determine how best to invest it. Without getting too deep into investing, strategy, rates of return, and risk, here are a few principles for investing and saving money:

have a plan
Always know why you're investing in something and stick to your plan.

understand your investment
Don't put money into anything unless you know what it is. I don't care if your parents give you investment advice, a stock broker tells you about a can't-miss opportunity, or you get a hot stock tip from your dog. Don't put money into something unless you understand it.

leave it alone
Don't invest in anything unless you are planning on leaving the money alone for at least five years. Otherwise you are just saving, not investing.

chapter twenty-five
how will I pay my bills?

Before you know it, you will venture out to your mailbox, only to find bills from various companies all expecting you to send them money. It's not quite as exciting as when Grandma sends you $5 for your birthday! When you're out on your own, especially if you're living in an apartment or a house, you will be amazed by the number of bills that come your way. Bills for Internet service, cell phone, home phone, car insurance, electricity, water, trash, cable, newspaper and magazine subscriptions, car payments, school loans, and credit cards are just a few of the bills that will come to visit you. Oh, and, of course, you have rent!

Paying your bills isn't rocket science, but you have to be disciplined with both your time and your money. There is a delicate tightrope you must walk, balancing the bills you owe and the money you have. Add in the obstacle that you only get paid at certain times of the month (weekly, biweekly, bimonthly), and your bills are due on different dates during the month, which can create some cash flow issues. Paying bills requires creating and sticking to a budget, so that when a bill is due, you have the money available to pay it.

So how do you actually pay your bills? Thankfully, it really isn't too difficult. Basically, you will get a bill in the mail saying that you owe a certain amount of money. You should always double check the bill to make sure it is accurate. Once every few months, I will find something wrong with a bill. It is usually not anything major, but you don't want to pay an extra $5 for a service you didn't order, right? The other key piece of information on a bill is the due date. Most companies will allow some extra time as a grace period, but try to get in the habit of paying all your bills early or on time. By doing this, you not only avoid getting killed with late fees (which can be anywhere from a few bucks to $50 with some credit card companies), but you are also establishing good credit. (We'll talk more about your credit in a few chapters.) Once you have checked this information, there are a couple of different ways you can actually pay the bill.

However you choose to pay your bills, you have to create a system for it. Do it the same way every time, so you don't send payments late, you always have the money to pay the bills, and, of course, you don't let bills go unpaid by letting them fall through the cracks. Some people write out a check when the bill arrives, stick it in an envelope, and put a sticky note on it with the date to drop it in the mail. Whenever I get a bill, I set it aside in a folder with the rest of the bills. Then once a week, I pull out any bills in that folder and pay them. This way I'm only paying bills a couple times each month and not every day. That is what works for me, but you have to determine what makes sense for you.

The other thing that I would highly recommend is to check with your bank to see if they have an online bill paying service. I use this with my bank and pay all my bills through this system. I just go online to the bank's website, log in, click which bills I want to pay, enter in the amount to pay and choose which date I want the bill to be paid on. When that date comes, the bank will either transfer the funds or mail a check to the company for me. How cool is that?!

Another option you may want to consider is having certain bills automatically drafted from your checking account. This means that on a specific date each month, the company you owe the money to will transfer a certain amount out of your checking account to cover that month's bill. This works extremely well if they bill you for the same amount each month and if it is always due on the same date. Once you set it up, it is automatic, and you don't have to stress about it. If you go this route, make sure you always have the money there on the date they make the withdrawal for the bill. If you don't have enough money in your account to cover the bill, the bank and the bill company will drill you with fees. The last thing you want to do is waste money on fees.

However you decide to pay your bills, develop a system and follow it. Here's the deal: if you don't pay a bill, the company will stop providing that service to you. If you don't pay your electricity bill, the utility company will turn your lights off. If you don't pay your cell phone bill, your phone will stop working some random day. If you don't pay your car payment, you will soon be walking everywhere! So get organized and pay your bills. (I don't want you to freeze to death in your own house because you didn't pay the heating bill!)

taxes: a necessary evil

As you may have already discovered, and will continue to learn as you get older, taxes are a necessary evil! You might as well get used to the government always taking a chunk of the money you make! It's a Catch-22: the more money you make, the more they take.

Welcome to the real world. Not always so fun is it?!

If you're in high school working a part time job, you probably realize that you're already paying income taxes whether you like it or not. Every time you get a paycheck from your employer, you've noticed there are large chunks of money missing from your check. Why? Very simply, the government wants their cut before you get yours. If you've had a job for over a year and have filed taxes, you've probably also noticed that most of the money the government takes is given back to you at the end of the year. Effective system, huh?!

The nutshell of taxes is this: in order to keep functioning, the government collects taxes in a variety of different forms. If you go to the store and buy something, you know you're going to pay sales tax on your purchase. At the same time, if you have a job, the government will withhold income tax from you. Of course, we all hate how much money we pay to the government, but it is just part of life. You may as well make your peace with it now.

One thing you may have learned is if you earn an income at all, you must file your income taxes for that year. When I say, "file your taxes" that means once a year, you fill out some paperwork to tell the government how much money you made and how much you owe them. Like I mentioned before, your employer will take a little bit out of each paycheck throughout the year. This prevents you from having to pay a big chunk of taxes at the end of year. By the way, you must file your taxes each year by April 15 for your previous year's income. For example, if you were filing your taxes for the income you made in 2008, you must file those forms with the government by April 15, 2009.

Your income tax is based on how much money you make. If you're working at a part time job, you will probably owe very little, if any, taxes at the end of the year. If your employer withheld your taxes from you, that amount will be given back when you file your taxes, which is known as a refund. As you get older and presumably make more money, the government will want a bigger and bigger piece of the pie. There are various tax brackets, so if you are single and make $25,000, your tax rate would be 15%. But if you make $50,000, your tax rate would jump to 25%. It is based on a sliding scale and again, will vary depending on your income.

One of the best things you can do now is be familiar with the process. If you're not a numbers person (or you have a headache after reading these first few paragraphs!), then find someone to help you with your taxes. Personally, I do my own taxes and have done so since I was a teenager. I have learned a lot in the process by doing them myself. Every year, I use a computer software program, which greatly simplifies the process. Of course, you can always figure your taxes using just the tax form and a pencil.

If you do your taxes yourself, make certain you know what you're doing. The government doesn't mess around when it comes to taxes. They don't care if you're a naïve 16 year old who has never filed taxes before. They just want to know exactly what you earned, so they make sure they get a chunk of that money. If you're off by a penny, they may not throw you in jail tomorrow but just understand how important it is to file your taxes accurately. Regardless of what your personal feeling is about taxes, it is still your responsibility as an American to pay them. As Benjamin Franklin once said, "In this world, nothing is certain but death and taxes." Ain't that the truth?

What you spend your **money** on doesn't define **who you are.**

is it okay to splurge on myself?

Picture this...you go to the mall with some friends planning to spend $50 on some new clothes. You browse around for a while until you find this pair of jeans that are perfect for you. Oddly enough, there is only one pair left, and they happen to be in your size. It's almost too good to be true, but there's only one problem. They cost $100; twice as much as you had planned to spend, right? You justify that it's still a great deal, and you rationalize that you just can't live without them! "I deserve it," you tell yourself. You work hard, so you should get to spend a little extra on yourself, shouldn't you? Of course you should.

On top of that, as you are walking up to pay for your "twice-as-much-as-you-should-spend" pair of jeans, you notice a shirt that would perfectly complete this outfit! It is on sale for only $35. What's another $35, right? Of course, at the counter you find a watch and a necklace that match your newly created outfit, and eventually you leave the store having spent way more than you expected. But you deserve it, right?!

If you don't have the money, you don't deserve it!

Now you may get a little laugh out of this story, but don't kid yourself...this happens every day with people just like you and me. We work hard all week, so we justify that we deserve to splurge a little on ourselves. It's our money, and we earned it, so we should be able to spend it how we want. But if you're not careful, you can very quickly waste a lot of money and rack up a lot of debt buying crap you don't need, all the while justifying how you deserve it.

So can you splurge on yourself a little? The simple answer is 'yes' and 'no'. Being able to splurge a little on yourself means something different to everyone. To one person, it may mean that instead of just getting a hamburger, you get the whole value meal! To someone else, splurging may mean that instead of buying one outfit, you buy the entire store! Obviously, there is a huge difference in how people view "splurging." Basically, if you have the money and you want to spend a little on yourself within reason, there is nothing wrong with that...*if* you have the money. But it is absolutely stupid to splurge on yourself with money you don't have, by putting something on a credit card. There are so many people in our culture who try to live a "Steak and Lobster Lifestyle" on a McDonald's budget! That doesn't work. You have to learn to live within your means. Here are three simple principles to help you do this:

don't splurge if you have debt

If you're in debt with car loans, school loans, or credit card debt, then now is not the time to be splurging. You've already created a mess, so why would you want to add to it? If you have any kind of debt, learn to delay gratification, make sacrifices, and you'll win long term. Which is more valuable? A quick spring break trip to Cancun today or having the ability to take several weeks of vacation anywhere in the world tomorrow? Dave Ramsey, a financial guru, always says, "If you live like no one else, later you will get to live like no one else." Chew on that.

if you are going to splurge, splurge proportionally to your finances

If you're a greeter at Wal-Mart (which would be an awesome job), and you make minimum wage, you probably can't afford to be taking ski trips to Switzerland! If you're going to splurge on something, it has to make sense for your finances. If you make $1,000 a month and you want to blow $200 on clothes, that's 20% of your income. But if you make $10,000 a month and you want to blow $200 on clothes, that's only 2% of your income. Which makes more sense?

splurging only produces a temporary feeling

For some people, the danger in splurging is that it produces a type of euphoric buzz. There is a certain rush of adrenaline and excitement when you buy a really nice outfit or eat at an ultra fancy restaurant. But remember, that is just temporary. If you're thinking about splurging on something, sleep on it, wait 24 hours, and then ask yourself if you really need it. This can help prevent you from making stupid decisions.

Let me stress one other key point here. What you spend your money on doesn't define who you are. If you need to, stop, go back, and reread that statement. What you spend your money on doesn't define who you are. I don't care how expensive your clothes are, how big your house is, what kind of car you drive, or how much money you make. All of those things are trivial compared to who you are as a person. If you catch anything from this chapter, make it this: don't splurge on crap just to impress other people. That is immature, shallow, and stupid. Chances are, the people who try to impress others with how they spend their money are probably in so much debt, they can't see the light of day. Don't be that person.

do I need insurance?

Yes.

Ok, let me give you at least a few more details about insurance. Like taxes, insurance is one of those necessary evils in life. You may feel like you're throwing money away with it, but if a disaster strikes, you're going to be really happy you have it. For the past number of years, you've probably been under your parents' various insurance policies, but at some point in the very near future, that will all come to an end. It is important to begin figuring out now, not only what insurance is, but why you need it, and what types of insurance you should have.

what is insurance?
When you purchase insurance, you pay money (known as a premium) to transfer risk from yourself to the insurance company. Let's take car insurance as an example. We all know that any time you get in a car and go for a drive, there is a chance you could get in an accident. The accident may be that an old lady behind you tapped your bumper or your car got hit by a train (you would rather deal with the old lady than the train!). If you're in an accident, and it requires $5,000 worth of repairs to your car, chances are you don't have $5,000

lying around waiting to fix your damaged car. This is where insurance comes in. Instead of spending $5,000 out of your pocket to fix the car, you buy auto insurance which helps to protect you. You pay a monthly premium, and in exchange, the insurance company will help pay for damages if the car is in an accident. This is the basic idea of insurance.

One other key insurance term you need to be familiar with is a deductible. Very simply, a deductible is the amount you have to pay first (above your monthly premiums) before your insurance coverage will kick in and pay for damages. Going back to our example above, if you have a $1,000 deductible on your car insurance, you have to pay that amount first and the insurance company will cover everything above that. It's important to note that this differs from one insurance company to the next in terms of what they cover after you pay your deductible. Make sure you fully understand your insurance policy. When it comes to your deductible, there is a simple equation insurance companies use:

High Deductibles = Lower Premiums
AND
Low Deductibles = Higher Premiums

If your deductible is $500, your monthly premium may be much higher than if your deductible was $2,500. You have to remember that your monthly premium is based on risk. A brand new, 16- year old driver is much more expensive to insure than a 45-year old who has never had a wreck. Obviously the 16-year old poses a much higher risk than the 45-year old, due to age and experience, so just remember that your premiums will be higher now than later.

do I need insurance?
You absolutely need and have got to have insurance. I know it's expensive. I know you're a great driver and you have perfect health, so it seems like a waste of money, but you must have

insurance. Insurance is there not for the small fender bender or a runny nose, but it's there to protect you from the major catastrophe that you don't see coming. You may be in perfect health today, but if you're in a freak accident that puts you in the hospital for a week, you could easily have over $100,000 in medical bills. Do you have $100,000 in cash ready for those situations? I didn't think so! One study showed the number one cause of bankruptcy, accounting for half of the bankruptcies in the US, was medical bills.[1] So yes, you must have insurance. Not for the little problems, but for the disastrous crisis that you least expect.

what kinds of insurance do I need?
You can get insurance coverage on just about anything but here are two types of insurance that everyone needs.

auto insurance
Insurance for your car is one type of insurance that isn't optional. In fact, it's the law. Like any other type of insurance, there are different levels and variations of car insurance, but the bottom line is, in most states it is illegal to drive without car insurance.

health insurance
Right now you're probably still under your parent's health insurance, but it would be a good idea to have them check at what age you will no longer be covered. Some policies cut you off at 18, others at 21, and still others may wait until you move out of the house. Once you're on your own, as I stressed before, you've got to get health insurance. Check with your employer, because many companies offer some type of insurance that is generally cheaper than what you can get on your own.

You may also look into renter's insurance (if you rent an apartment or a house) and life insurance (depending if you are married or have children). Find a reputable insurance agent in your area to discuss what types of insurance you need for your current situation.

Not to beat a dead horse (I wonder if the horse had life insurance?), but you have to make sure your bases are covered when it comes to insurance. If a disaster strikes in your life, you want to be prepared, and insurance is one way to make that happen.

chapter twenty-nine
should I be concerned about identity theft?

Unless you've been living in a cave for the past several years (that would be cool...no pun intended), you've probably seen or heard something in the news about a growing problem known as identity theft. Whether you realize it or not, this is becoming a huge crisis in America, and it is certainly something you should be aware of. To start with, let's clarify exactly what identity theft is.

Basically, identity theft is when thieves steal your personal information and pretend to be you, usually for financial gain. They can use this form of fraud in a variety of ways. They may use your personal information to open a new credit card account and charge it up, all while pretending to be you. They may gain access to your banking information and clean out your accounts. Identity theft can take several different forms, but the thing you need to realize is how common this has become. MSNBC reports that one in twelve people will become a victim of identity theft.

The biggest pain about identity theft is cleaning up the mess the thief left behind. If he has your personal information and pretends to be you, he will probably be charging up credit cards, opening new accounts and buying random junk. You're then stuck trying to convince all those places where the thief made purchases that it wasn't really you in the first place. That's not my idea of a good time. A study shows that victims now spend an average of 600 hours recovering from this crime, which represents nearly $16,000 in lost potential income.[1]

So how does someone even go about stealing your identity? Identity theft generally starts with how you handle your personal information, such as your name, Social Security number, credit card numbers, or other financial account information. If an identity thief can get their hands on this info, they have hit the jackpot. You should also know that a high majority of identity theft cases involve a close friend or family member who may have easy access to your personal information.

Other than family members, friends, or general misuse of your information, here are other ways that identity thieves work:

data theft
Since 2005, over 200 million people have had their identities stolen through corporate data theft. This happens when identity thieves gain access to customer records for major businesses and corporations. One example of data theft occurred when nearly 46 million identities were stolen from corporate giant, TJ Maxx.

stealing
Thieves are looking for anything where they can get your personal information. Wallets, purses, mail (including bank and credit card statements), pre-approved credit offers, tax information, or even job and personnel records.

phishing
You may have encountered this online before; identity thieves pretending to be financial institutions or companies by sending spam or pop-up messages to get you to reveal your personal

information. This is extremely common online, and you should always be heads up for this.

changing your address
Sometimes identity thieves will fill out a change of address form so that your personal mail starts getting directed to a new address. Then the thieves can begin collecting your mail and going through your personal information.

So how do you avoid this happening to you? Here are some ideas:

pay attention
The best thing you can do is just to keep an eye on your finances and your personal information for anything out of the ordinary. If anything suspicious happens such as missing checks from your checkbook, not receiving your bank or credit card statement in the mail, or getting a call from a collection agency about a charge you didn't make, a red flag should go off in your head.

be a shredding machine
Of course there are certain files and documents that you must save, but for everything else, shred it. First of all, let's be honest...shredding stuff is really kind of fun. Don't deny it. If there is anything that has any personal information on it that you don't need to keep for any reason, shred it immediately. And enjoy!

be skeptical
If you get a random call from someone asking for your personal information, don't give it to him. If you get an email that is asking for personal data, delete the email. Don't roll the dice on something like identity theft.

If you ever think you are a victim of identity theft, there are several things you should do immediately:

file a police report

If someone stole your car, you would let the police know right away, wouldn't you? File a police report, and keep a copy of the report for your records.

check your credit report

Your credit report is a listing of your current debt and your debt history. There are three major credit bureaus that keep track of this: Experian (www.experian.com), Equifax (www.equifax.com), and Trans Union (www.transunion.com). If you notice anything suspicious on your credit report, you should put a fraud alert on your report. You can do this by going to the individual credit bureau websites.

cancel any suspicious accounts

If you think someone got your bank information, close that account and switch banks. Notify the bank or the organization, so they will be heads up to anything suspicious. If your purse or wallet is stolen, cancel any type of account or card immediately that a thief may then have access to. Also, put a "stop payment" on all lost or stolen checks and cards.

You don't need to live in fear everyday that someone will steal your identity, but you should be aware that it is just as likely to happen to you as it is to anyone else. Pay attention, be smart, and you should be fine. But even then, in the unlikely situation that your identity is stolen, do whatever you need to do to get the mess cleaned up immediately.

do I need to get a credit card?

Quite honestly, a credit card is probably not the best thing for a student to have, especially a student with no money! This means pretty much all students, then, since they're usually all broke! I think as you look at credit cards as a whole, you will find that the bad far outweighs the good. For example, did you know that the average cardholder carries an $8,562 balance on his or her card from month to month, paying an average of 18.3% in interest?[1] That amounts to $929.70 a year in interest payments. Think of this: if you took that $929.70 that you could pay just in interest alone and invested that over a 40 year period with a 12% average return, you would end up with over $920,000!

Our society thinks debt is just a part of life. As I've said before, our culture expects you will always have a car loan, credit card bill, or a student loan payment. They tell you once you get into debt, there's nothing you can do - you're just stuck there forever. That's the stupidest thing I've ever heard.

If you think you have to have a credit card, let me at least give you a few things to consider:

high interest rates

Credit cards are known to have some of the highest and most ridiculous interest rates of any type of lender. Seventy-two percent of credit cards have a variable interest rate, meaning your interest rate can change on a regular basis. Plus, virtually all credit cards today have a provision in the contract that essentially says they can raise your interest rate at any time, for any reason, without warning. It's called the Universal Default Provision, and it is in the fine print of any credit card agreement you sign. Look it up. It's there.

"gotcha" fees

Credit cards have all kinds of ridiculous fees for just about anything and everything you can think of. They can gouge you if you're a day late on your payment or if you spend more than your credit limit. These fees can be anywhere from $20 to as much as $50. With some cards, there are also transaction fees for calling the "toll-free" number to check your balance and penalty fees if you haven't used your card in awhile and your account has been inactive. In a study done by Georgetown University, they found that college students tend to make late payments and exceed their credit limits more frequently than other age groups and therefore incur more fees than other groups.[2]

emotional strain

Any time you have debt, it feels like a big weight you carry around. In a very real sense, you are a slave to whomever you owe that money to. Every time you collect a paycheck, a good chunk of that money is going to pay your debt; you always end up working for someone else as opposed to working for yourself. A study by the American Bankruptcy Institute reveals that 19% of the people who filed for bankruptcy last year were college students, and that 69% of bankruptcy filers said credit card debt caused the bankruptcy. Never underestimate the emotional and mental toll that debt will have on your life.

When it comes to the dangers of credit cards, most people will have one of these common responses:

"it's only for emergencies"

This is why we mentioned earlier that you have to create an emergency fund. If you have an rainy day fund in place, there is no need to have a credit card for emergencies.

"I get reward points"

If you were to ask a millionaire what the secret to financial success is, do you really think they would say that they made their millions on Discover reward points?! *Consumer Reports* says that 75% of the airline miles earned through credit cards are never even redeemed. If you step back and think about what you are really getting for how you use your credit card, it's absolutely ridiculous. One of the biggest targets for credit card companies is college students. One gimmick that companies use to attract students is giving out a free t-shirt for signing up for a new card. Think about that for a second. Wow. The opportunity to go into debt for a t-shirt?! Do I even need to tell you how stupid that sounds?

"I pay it off each month"

According to CardTrak.com, 60% of people don't pay off their credit cards every month. Which makes me wonder...do you think that the 60% of people who don't pay off their cards had the same idea as you? They probably thought they would just pay it off each month, too – no big deal. Until life happened. And they were late a day, and the credit card company tacked on a nice little fee they hadn't planned on. Or they lost track of how much they put on the card that month and when the bill came, they only paid the minimum payment. This is far too common. On top of that, a study by Dunn and Bradstreet shows that credit card users spend 12% - 18% more when using credit instead of cash. Paying off your credit card balance each month sounds nice in theory, but it doesn't always work like you plan.

Each year *Forbes* magazine publishes a list of the 400 richest people in America. When the magazine surveyed this group of "bazillionaires," 75% of them said the best way to build wealth is to become and stay debt free! Some of the biggest companies in the country are debt free, such as Walgreens, Cisco, Microsoft, and Harley-Davidson. In reality, credit cards are a dangerous game of roulette, and I don't know if you want to take that chance.

should I be trying to build my credit?

You may have heard this before or even asked yourself this question, but the idea that you need to "build credit" is really kind of silly when you think about it. When people say they need to "build credit," they are referring to their credit score, which is also known as the FICO score. Your credit score is a three-digit number that serves as a measurement for banks, credit card companies, and other lending organizations to help them determine how reliable you will be to pay back money you borrow. The higher your score, the more likely you will be to pay back money you owe. If you have a lower score, it may mean that you paid a bill late in the past, perhaps you've filed for bankruptcy, or maybe you owe some money that you never even bothered to repay. Here is a breakdown for how your credit score is figured:

35% payment history
30% amount of debt
15% length of credit history
10% type of debt
10% applying for new credit

If you look through each of these factors that combine to make up your credit score, they all have one thing in common: DEBT! Your credit score is all based on how well you can borrow money and pay it back. It is a score based on how much you love debt! Are you beginning to see how stupid this seems? So if you have a salary of $5 million per year, no debt, and $20 million in the bank, you may have a really low credit score simply because you are debt free. So in reality, the higher your credit score, the better you are at acquiring and repaying debt. Is that really what you want to be financially known for?

If you've been paying attention to anything you've read in this section so far, you probably picked up on the fact that if you want to succeed financially, you've got to learn to stay out of debt. Having a good credit score is NOT an indication of wealth or success. As I mentioned in the previous chapter, some of the richest people in America say the key to wealth is living debt free. This means that all of their credit scores probably suck! Hopefully, you're beginning to see that a crappy credit score may be a good thing!

You may wonder then how you buy a car or a house. If you need to buy a car, you need to be diligent enough to save up and pay cash for it. This is what my wife and I do, and we have never regretted it. I will admit that a house is a little different monster. Ideally, it would be great if you could save up and pay cash for a house, but I'm realistic enough to know that most people, especially young adults in their twenties, would have a tough time pulling this off. If you need to get a loan for a house, there are ways to get one without needing a credit score. You will have to go to a mortgage company or lender that does what is called "manual underwriting." This is when a lender looks at you, as an individual, to make a decision about lending you money for a mortgage, as opposed to making a lending decision based solely on a three-digit number (which any monkey could do!). If you are considering "manual underwriting," here are some common factors lenders will look at to determine if you qualify for a mortgage:

• You have paid your landlord early or on time for two years.

• You have no other credit or debt.

• You have a solid down payment - nothing down is not solid.

• You have been in the same career field for two years.

• You are not trying to bite off more than you can chew. Your payment on your mortgage should be no more than 25% of your take-home pay. If you make $2,000 a month and request a loan with a payment of $1,200 month...good luck.

As you have probably figured out, lenders want to see that you are a stable, normal person, and that you're not going to wig out on them. In reality, if you can still qualify for a mortgage without a credit score, and if you plan on paying for everything else in cash, then I guess that defeats the purpose of trying to build your credit score, doesn't it?

the real world:
it's not like MTV

chapter thirty-two
HELP! I'm afraid of the real world!

Do you remember the first day of kindergarten? You had this feeling that was a mix of "This is going to be awesome," and "I hope I don't pee my pants!" You probably had the same emotional roller coaster your first day of middle school, and maybe even high school. You had that feeling when you got your driver's license, too, didn't you? I remember experiencing that wave of emotion during all of those moments of life, not to mention when I got married and became a father.

Each time we open a new chapter in the stories of our lives, it becomes very difficult to know what is next. If you're in high school and are getting ready to graduate, the past few years could probably be described as comfortable. Why? Because you know how everything works. You know what you can and can't get away with in class. You've established a solid foundation of friends that you probably spend most of your time with. And for the most part, you think you've got life pretty much figured out up to this point.

But when you make that transition from high school to college and the real world, suddenly you are entering into the land of the unknown. The first day you went to kindergarten, you were excited for this new adventure, but you were terrified because you weren't entirely sure what you were supposed to be doing. You may have that same feeling now. You're completely excited that you're growing up, becoming an adult, and will soon experience more freedom than you've ever had. But inside, there's a freaked-out little kid who wants to sit in the corner, rock back and forth, suck his thumb, and be held by Mommy. (That's a pretty picture, isn't it?)

Let's be honest. It is easier to stay in a situation that you are comfortable in than to venture out into the unknown. It's easier to stay on the shore as opposed to jumping in the ocean. There is a fear that you don't know what's in the ocean or if you'll be able to swim. But if you always stay on the shore, you'll never experience the feeling of playing in the ocean. Besides, if you get freaked out, you can always pee in the ocean. Nobody will know the difference.

The point is this: on the first day of anything, you're freaked out and are probably sensing a minor anxiety attack. But after a while, you kind of figure things out, don't you? Over the first few weeks, you got the hang of kindergarten, and it wasn't too bad. One of my first weeks, I learned that you're not supposed to pull someone's chair out from underneath them. Prior to kindergarten, supposedly I didn't know that. I learned this is frowned upon. You figured out the game in high school, too, and thankfully you managed to navigate your way through. College and the real world are exactly the same way. At first, you're scared out of your mind, but over time you'll figure it out.

It is all just part of the journey of growing up. While it may seem simpler and more convenient to sit on the shore for the rest of your life, that's no way to live. It's fine to be a little nervous about the future, but don't pee your pants over it (unless you're in the ocean). Eventually you'll figure it out, and get the hang of things. It's all part of the experience of growing up and becoming an adult. It's kind of like a reality check, isn't it? (That would make a great book title!).

People work their entire lives to **obtain** status, titles, things, and money, but if your quality of life sucks, then **is it worth it?**

work, school, activities, life... how do I balance it all?

Balancing everything that you have going on in life is a continual struggle. You have a limited amount of time, energy, and resources and an unlimited amount of opportunities where you can spend them. So how do you balance it all? Is it even realistic to have balance, or is it just a big myth? Here are some key ideas to keep in mind:

determine what matters most

As you are pulled in countless directions, you should begin to determine what matters most to you. Without taking the time to first answer this question, then everything is important and nothing is important all at the same time. One thing you might consider is creating a personal mission statement to help guide you. Companies and organizations have mission statements that help define who they are and what they are about. By having a personal mission statement, you can better define what matters and what doesn't in your life.

create boundaries

Here is a great word to add to your vocabulary that you need to start using frequently: NO! This is a word that you have to get good at using in order to maintain any sense of balance. If you create a mission statement, then you can use this as a tool to set boundaries in your life. Creating boundaries will give you the ability to say 'no' to the things that you just can't do.

you are not a machine
As young and active as we are (you more so than me), we still have our limits. If you work 60 hours a week, take a full load of classes, stay involved in all your clubs and activities, keep up with your homework, and try to have some friendships along the way, you are going to kill yourself. You have limits and a capacity to what you're capable of doing, so remind yourself of that when you think you're a machine.

stop and smell the roses
Life is too short to just work, work, work, and then fall over and die. I want to enjoy life along the way, don't you? That means you have to build in fun, recreation, and downtime along the way. Most students don't have a problem with this, but as you continue into the real world, it will become more and more difficult. Don't become too consumed with the busyness of life that you forget to stop and smell the roses.

who you are is more important than what you do
I use this phrase all the time, and I believe it whole-heartedly. Unfortunately though, we live in a culture that values possessions and titles over people. Think about when you first meet someone, what is one of the first questions you ask: "So, what do you do for a living?" And immediately people will make assumptions about you based solely on what you do. Whether you are the CEO or the janitor, who you are will always be more important than what you do.

balance doesn't naturally happen
As you may have figured out by now, balance doesn't just happen. It is something you have to be extremely proactive

about working for. There will always be opportunities to spend more time than what you have available. You have to set up those boundaries and determine what you are going to do differently. Think through some practical, proactive things you can do to begin to achieve balance in your own life.

This is one of the most important chapters in this book because so few of us are good at balance. People work their entire lives to obtain status, fancy titles, nice things, and lots of money, but if your quality of life sucks and you are just a shell of a human being, is it really worth it? That is no way to live life. On your death bed someday, will you be concerned about what kind of car you drove and what brand your clothes were? Or will you be thinking about the memories you created with the people you love the most? Make it a priority now to work towards balance.

should I vote?
who should I vote for?

Voting on issues and for political leaders is not only one of your rights but also one of your responsibilities as an American. Many students have legitimate questions about voting that I will address:

why?
One of the biggest concerns that students have about the voting process is if their vote even matters. "Does it really make a difference whether or not I vote?" we often ask. But if every person had that mindset and no one voted, then the democratic system that we have would no longer work. Your vote will be counted, so why wouldn't you want to have your say in the process? Many countries around the world don't have a democratic system. Their governmental leaders and officials are decided for them regardless of viewpoints and belief systems. By voting, you have the opportunity to let your voice be heard. If you are not happy with the elected officials that are in place, you have as much power as anybody else to do something about it. But if you are not happy with the way things are and you did not vote, then you don't have any reason to say anything.

who?

The next challenge is figuring out who to vote for. In politics, there are two major voting parties you have probably heard about: Republicans and Democrats. Republicans tend to be more conservative on political issues, while Democrats tend to be more liberal. Each of the individuals who make up these political parties has a general set of beliefs and values that they tend to lean towards. In addition, there are some officials who do not associate themselves with either party and are known as Independents. In an election, your responsibility is to figure out not only who you think would do the best job in that elected role, but also which candidate most closely reflects your beliefs and opinions. If you're going to vote for someone, wouldn't you prefer to vote for someone who closely mirrors how you personally think?

when?

There are many different types of elections on many different levels. There are local, city, county, state, and national elections. Some elections are an opportunity to vote for a candidate for a certain political position, and other elections are for you to vote on specific issues in the area such as a tax increase for a community development project. Elections can happen throughout the year, but most major elections happen in November. The Presidential election happens in November every four years.

where?

Before you can vote anywhere, you have to meet two simple qualifications: 1) You must be at least 18 years old, and 2) you must register to vote. To register to vote, contact your local city or town hall to see what the process is. You may need to go to the city hall to fill out a form, sometimes they can mail you the form, and some areas are going to an online voter registration system. Regardless, in most states you are required to register at least 30 days prior to an election. After you have completed that process you will receive a voter registration card that will show you where you will actually cast your vote. It is normally a community location such as a school or church that is close to where you live.

Every year there is a growing interest in the election process among young people. Candidates, especially in presidential elections, are targeting young voters because they make up such a large voting demographic. In addition, more and more young people are getting involved with political campaigns in order to attract more voters for their chosen candidate. This is a great way to get involved with the political process and to encourage others to get involved as well.

Let me provide one additional thought on the issue of voting. While you have the responsibility to vote and help select our nation's governing officials, it's important to remember that no one you elect is going to change your life. So often we look to the President or Congress or the government in general to take care of us and solve our problems. And while part of their responsibility is to protect you as an American citizen, very little that they actually do in Washington D.C. will have a direct impact on your day to day life.

Too many people count on the government to fix their lives when in reality; you must learn to take personal responsibility for your own decisions and the outcomes. While some elected officials are certainly better than others in bringing about change, the only person who can truly change your life is you.

how do I find a place to live?

Living on your own is one of the most exciting parts of growing up. For years, you've lived with Mom and Dad, and now you're ready to spread your wings and leave the nest. The challenge is now you have to find another "nest" to live in. Living on your own can seem really appealing, but once you actually get out on your own, it is also easy to realize how good you had it living with your parents. (You probably never imagined you would have that thought!) Let's explore some options, and the pros and cons of each:

live in the dorms

If you're taking a full load of classes in college, living on campus in the dorms is a great option for you. If you're living in the dorms, you are probably within walking distance of everywhere you would need to be, depending on the size of the campus. This obviously saves you money on gas. Of course if you're not a very social person, and you like to go to bed at 9.30 each night, dorm life may not be a good fit for you. Also, determine how much you will actually utilize the meal plan that may come with living in the dorms. It's always a good idea to do the math for what the room and board fee is, and figure out what it actually costs to live in the dorms on a monthly basis. Compare this to your other options from a financial standpoint.

rent an apartment / house

Renting either an apartment or a house fairly close to campus is a very common option for college students. If you're a campus socialite, living off campus may give you the feeling of being disconnected from everything, however, you will definitely have more peace and quiet than what the dorm offers. Plus you will likely have more space than your average dorm room. Of course, you have a new level of financial responsibility when renting. While some rentals offer an all-inclusive monthly cost, most require that you pay certain utilities such as electric, water, or cable which can get expensive. In addition, you have to pay your rent to your landlord every month, so you better have the money when rent is due. One upside to a rental is that you are usually not responsible for routine repair and maintenance expenses.

A great way to help offset some of this expense is to share it with roommates. If you do end up with roommates, make sure they are people you trust and enjoy being around (they will be there a lot!). Also, make sure you establish up front some ground rules and what your agreement will be on certain issues. For example, who pays for groceries? Will you split all monthly expenses evenly? What happens if you need to go to bed but they want to have friends over? Once you establish this agreement, make sure you put it in writing, have all of you sign it, and keep that document filed away.

buy a house

Although this may seem like the most appealing option, it has the most risks for students. The common assumption is that if you are living in an apartment and paying rent, you are throwing money away. But if you buy a house, you know your monthly payment is actually going towards something. While this sounds nice in theory, there are so many more risks associated with owning a house that it can become a curse instead of a blessing. When you own a house, you are responsible for everything. If the water heater goes out, you're fixing it. If the roof has a leak, you're paying for it. If anything goes wrong, it falls back on you. Plus you have the added expense of home-owners insurance and property taxes. Having said all of that, here are a couple of criteria to have in place before buying a house.

• Be Debt Free – You don't need other payments and bills to add to the burden of owning a home.

• Have An Emergency Fund – This is that rainy day fund for the repairs and upkeep expenses you will have.

• Put As Much Down As Possible – The more you put as a down payment on the house, the less risk you have for yourself.

• Get a Fixed Interest Rate – You should avoid getting a mortgage with a variable interest rate. These can fluctuate too much and backfire on you.

stay at home
The least appealing, but perhaps the most practical option for housing, is just staying put with your folks. I know this sounds as exciting as watching grass grow, but it may very well be worth it. If they live even remotely close to where you will be going to school, your added gas expense is more than offset by little to no living expenses. Don't just assume you have a free ride, but any contribution you make to the living expenses of staying at home will be far less than living on your own. Is it the most attractive option? Maybe not. Is it the most sensible? Probably.

So where do you go from here? There are several factors to consider when finding a place to live:

proximity

Take into consideration how close your place will be to everywhere else you live life, including school, your job, your friends' places, and, of course, the nearest Wal-Mart. If you have really low rent, but you have to drive 45 minutes to get anywhere you need to go, is it worth it?!

finances

When looking for a place to live, you don't want to bite off more than you can chew financially. As you consider the financial side of the equation, think through the worst-case scenarios. If you have roommates and they decide to move out one day, can you still afford the place? Once you move in, what do you need to buy in order to make the place livable? Think these things through.

stage of life

Consider how permanent you want this place to be based on where you're at in life. If you are planning a major move in the next year, you probably don't want to be locked into a lengthy lease or anything remotely permanent. Think through possible job relocations, family, relationships or other situations that may cause you to move relatively soon.

area of town

In every city, there are areas of town where you would feel comfortable leaving your front door open at night. There are other places where you couldn't pay someone to live. Consider not only how safe and secure you will feel in an area but also how much peace and quiet you'll get.

chapter thirty-six
how can I find a mentor?

Finding and learning from a mentor (or several mentors for that matter) is one of the smartest things you can do. A mentor is someone who can speak into your life and provide you with insight, wisdom, and feedback. He acts as part advisor, part role model, part counselor, and part friend. The biggest advantage you have in finding a mentor is that you are young and have a desire to learn. Anybody who is successful has probably had mentors in his or her life. As a result, people you look up to and admire are generally very willing to help you out, especially since you are a young person.

Before you start searching for a mentor or placing an ad on Craigslist for one, you should first determine what you need a mentor for. You may want a mentor in your field of interest who can help you further develop your professional skills in that industry. You may want a mentor who can help you personally in areas such as relationships, finances, or just answer general questions about life. Once you determine what you're looking for, it will be easier to know where to look. Keep in mind that just because someone is successful in the business you are interested in, doesn't mean he would be a good mentor. Some people who are successful in business are just complete jerks and would make a horrible mentor. Here are some places to consider as you look:

current job

If you're in a job you love, and you have a great relationship with your boss, this is a great step towards finding a mentor. There may also be co-workers or colleagues who have been in the business for many years, and have tons of advice and experience they would be willing to share.

family & friends

One of your best ways of finding a quality mentor is by searching your own network of contacts. A mentor could be a family friend, a parent of one of your friends, someone your parents work with, or maybe a pastor at your local church.

google magic

I don't mean actually Google the word "magic," but rather take advantage of the Internet as a resource in finding a possible mentor. Many larger companies offer formal mentoring programs. You can also find organizations and associations that are designed to help connect potential mentors with students like yourself.

Once you find a mentor, here are some simple ideas that will keep the relationship strong:

discuss expectations

Before you begin any type of formal mentoring relationship with someone, it is a good idea to communicate to him exactly what it is you're looking for in a mentor, so he knows what he's getting into. By being clear about this up front, it prevents frustration and annoyance in the future.

ask questions like there's no tomorrow

Every time you get together with your mentor, you should have a list of questions that can guide the discussion. Don't expect him to show up with a PowerPoint presentation of what you're going to talk about. You initiated this relationship, so you need to take charge.

talk as little as possible

You're there to learn everything possible, so when you ask all your questions, shut up and let him answer! Sometimes you may feel the need to tell him about every little detail in your life, but in reality, you don't. You ask the questions, let him do the talking, and write down everything valuable he says.

be open to feedback

If you're there to learn, then be open to feedback and constructive criticism. Depending on the nature of your mentoring relationship, you came to this person because you respected who he is and what he does, so allow him to speak into your life without getting all bent out of shape.

show your appreciation

A mentoring relationship is a big commitment from both parties, but especially from the mentor. Show him you appreciate his time by being punctual, polite, and even paying for the meal if you go out to eat. Also, send him a thank you card. You will be amazed at what a handwritten card will do.

be a mentor to someone

If someone is willing to give back to you, then you can pay it forward to someone else. Look for others who you could mentor, and when the opportunity presents itself, give sacrificially of yourself to the other person. Someone did the same for you.

In my opinion, one of the best ways to learn anything is by learning from other people. If you want to be successful in life, figure out what successful people do, and do that. There is no need to reinvent the wheel here. However, you will never have the chance to "pick the brain" of someone you admire or respect unless you first ask him. Take advantage of the opportunity to learn from others. It starts by simply asking, and you won't know unless you ask.

do I need a resume?

You absolutely need a resume. A resume is basically a marketing piece that you use to sell yourself as an employee to the companies and organizations that you are interested in working for. A resume is a quick snap shot of not only your skills and abilities as an employee, but also the quality of person that you are. There are several elements that your resume needs to include:

contact information
Assuming they like you (which hopefully they will!) and want to move forward in the interview process, it would probably be helpful for them if they had a way to contact you! Make sure you provide all the necessary information including your full name, mailing address, home phone, cell phone, and email address. They probably won't need your MySpace or Facebook page info. Of course if you send them a friend request and they deny you, it's not looking good for you!

education history
I know you aced kindergarten, and second grade was the best three years of your life, but employers don't really care much about what you did in elementary or even in middle school. What they want to see is how you did in high school and college.

Remember that you're trying to stand out, so mention anything that sets you apart such as a good GPA or a high class rank. You might leave out that your favorite subjects were lunch and recess.

work experience
Here you can include any type of work experience you've had including part-time jobs, volunteer work, or internships. Employers aren't looking for potential employees who just talk a big game about what they *could* do, but they want students who have the experience to back it up. If you haven't had many jobs in the past, you can still demonstrate your skills with other experiences including involvement in your local church, leadership in clubs, or businesses that you've been involved with (i.e. babysitting or mowing lawns). Simply look for ways to show how you've displayed high levels of responsibility.

applicable skills
Especially if you are applying for a technical job, include any type of skills you have such as knowledge of software programs, computer systems, office equipment, or programming and design skills. You might want to leave out some of your lesser known talents such as your nunchuck skills, your ability to sleep for days at a time, or your unhealthy fascination with fire.

relevant categories
Depending on what type of job you are applying for, you may want to consider adding another category to show any related awards, significant achievements, leadership roles you've held, or just a paragraph of why you're so awesome.

Once you have compiled all of these elements into a resume format, here are a couple of other tips to remember when putting it all together:

one size doesn't fit all
Each job you apply for will be slightly different than the next. This makes it very difficult to have a one-stop resume that fits

what everyone is looking for. Take the time to customize your resume to the job. If you apply for a web programming job, bulk up the section about your programming skills and experience. If you're applying for a less technical job, they may not care as much about your expertise in that area.

K.I.S.S. (Keep It Simple, Stupid)
There is no need to write a small novel about your life and how great you are. Keep it short, sweet and to the point. Your resume really shouldn't be any longer than one or two pages. This is more than enough space to communicate the main points and will help you cut out all the excess junk that an employer won't care about. Anything longer than two pages may never even get read by potential employers.

remember to proofread
You would think this would be common sense, wouldn't you?! And yet still, there are always resumes people submit to potential employers that have typos. If you're an employer, and you receive a resume that is littered with typos, does that make you want to hire that person? Ov kors nott! So take the time to do more than Spell Check; print it out, and go over it with a fine-tooth comb.

always include a cover letter
A cover letter is the perfect way to introduce yourself to the potential employer and be able to express your interest in the job. This will be the first thing they read from you, so keep in mind the old saying, "You never get a second chance to make a first impression." Take the time to write a clear and personalized cover letter that makes them intrigued by you, before they ever see your resume.

If you're applying for a job with a pool of other applicants, your cover letter and resume may be the only tools you have to stand out from the competition. No matter what your little sister says, a glitter-covered resume will not help you stand out. Take the time to do it right, and do it with excellence.

how should I avoid screwing up a job interview?

Well first of all, congratulations that you even got the interview. Hopefully that means your resume was halfway decent, as we discussed in the previous chapter!

Now that we're to the interview stage of the process, there are some simple things you can do to avoid completely making a fool of yourself. Wear deodorant. Don't say "yes, sir" or "no, sir" if you're being interviewed by a woman. Limit the cussing from that potty mouth of yours. Don't belch. You know, just the usual public manners stuff that your mommy taught you. In fact, just to encourage you, here are some actual blunders that people have had during a job interview: [1]

• The candidate answered her cell phone and asked the interviewer to leave her own office because it was a "private" conversation.

• The candidate asked the interviewer for a ride home after the interview.

• When an applicant was offered food before the interview, he declined saying he didn't want to line his stomach with grease before going out drinking.

• The candidate flushed the toilet while talking to interviewer during a phone interview.

• The candidate took out a hair brush and brushed her hair during the interview.

To avoid being any of these people, here are some tips to help you with your interview:

prepare, prepare, prepare

Think of a job interview like a final exam in school. If you cram for it the night before and drink a couple of cases of Red Bull to keep you going, you're probably going to be a disaster come test time. But if you take the time to study and prepare, you can go in feeling calm, cool, and collected. Plus, your eyes won't be twitching from the caffeine buzz.

So how do you prepare? Think through possible questions they might ask and how you will respond. Google the company and learn everything you can, not only about the organization, but also about the person interviewing you. Practice actually saying what you want to communicate in the interview. Review your resume and know what points you want to highlight. Basically, just take the time to be prepared. A potential employer knows if you are taking this opportunity seriously or if you're just wasting their time. And do I really have to remind you to be on time?! You should actually plan to be early. Don't risk issues such as traffic, parking problems, or just general time management issues.

dress the part

A survey of over 3,000 hiring managers by CareerBuilder.com found that more than half, 51 percent, said the biggest mistake a potential candidate can make during an interview is dressing inappropriately.[2] Leave the bling at home and lean more towards the conservative side. Wear clean and professional clothes and don't overdo it with the accessories. This means you probably shouldn't wear that Superman t-shirt you got at the local thrift shop for a nickel. No cleavage, no navels, no butt cracks!

don't blame the past

In that same survey by CareerBuilder.com, they found that the second biggest mistake an applicant can make in an interview is talking negatively about a current or former employer. This communicates a bad attitude and perhaps sends the message that you are difficult to work with. While you don't need to sugar-coat everything and say that every boss and every job you've had have been perfect, don't spend the entire interview railing on the past.

follow up

You may not realize it, but the interview doesn't end after you walk out the door. After the interview, always send a handwritten thank you card or letter. The interviewer didn't have to take the time to talk with you, so show your appreciation for her time but also reiterate your interest in the position. Also, take the time after an interview to evaluate how you did. It probably won't be your last interview ever, so determine what went well and some areas for improvement for next time around.

be you

The biggest thing you have to do in an interview is be you. (Wow, that rhymed a lot.) An employer wants to meet the real you, not some imaginary person that you try to present yourself as. They want to hire an actual person, so you have to show them what they are getting. While you may try to present yourself as what you think they are looking for, in reality, they just want to get to know the real you. So be you in the interview. (I did it again.)

what should I ask in a job interview?

It's important to remember that a job interview isn't just about them quizzing you. It is also a chance for you to get to know them as a company. You may be totally pumped about a particular job, only to find out that the potential boss, who interviewed you, is a jerk.

Once you actually get into the interview itself, sometimes your nerves may get the best of you, and you think your only role is to answer their questions. While you, of course, want to put your best foot forward and try to make a solid impression, don't miss out on the opportunity to conduct an interview of them. Hopefully, you're not so mentally drained from their pop quiz that you don't ask any questions of your own.

By asking them some questions, you are also communicating your level of interest in the position. You are letting them know that you are not there to just go through the formality of the interview, but that you are genuinely interested in this opportunity. Here are 10 good questions to toss out there:

if I do an outstanding job in my role, what would that look like?
This will help you define expectations a little better. Your understanding of "success" in the new role may be completely different than your boss'. Be clear up front about expectations and always get it in writing before the job begins. It's also a good idea to ask the opposite question: "If I'm a complete disaster, what would that look like?"

what do you like best about working here?
The person interviewing you was once in the same position that you're in now. Obviously she's done something right and has been there for a decent length of time, so it would be interesting to hear her perspective on the company. Is she positive and upbeat about the organization, or does she spend a lot of time ripping the company?

what are you passionate about?
This question will help you learn a little more about your potential boss. While some people would advise against this type of question, the reality is that people want to work with people they like. Use discretion when asking this question, but it can help determine if you like your potential boss, and she will determine if she likes you.

what types of advancement and growth opportunities are available here?
If the job you are interviewing for offers no room for growth, you should take that into consideration. If you've already hit the glass ceiling before you even start, is that really a job you want? Determine what kind of opportunities there are for moving into management or other roles that interest you.

what is the average day / week like in my role?

This helps you get a good idea of what you'll actually be doing on a day to day basis. Are you working with others or by yourself? Is your job more people-oriented or task-oriented? You get the idea.

what is the company culture like?

You have to ask yourself if this is a place you really want to work at. If you're casual and laid back, but you notice everyone is in suits and ties, nobody smiles, and joking is not permitted, is that the type of culture you want to work in? But if you're very serious and professional, then their Slurpee machine in the break room, spontaneous Wiffle ball tournaments in the office, and attire of shorts and flip flops could be concerning to you.

what is your leadership style?

You should consider what kind of boss you want to work for. Does the boss seem to be more of a micromanager who is always in your business? Or does she come across as more hands off and allow you room to breathe, but perhaps may not provide much feedback or instruction.

is there anything I should ask you that I haven't already asked?

This is a great question. This will tell them that you're serious about the job, and it will also show how honest they are willing to be with you.

where do we go from here?

By asking this, I don't mean you're checking to see if she wants to go grab a bite for lunch or if she wants to catch a movie! Do you have another interview with her or someone else? Do you have to fill out additional paperwork? Will she be contacting you once they've made the decision, either good or bad? You should get a clear idea of what the next step will be.

can I contact you if I think
of other questions?

A question like this keeps the door open for future communication with them. Again, it also reminds them that you are very interested in the opportunity. Don't take this as an invitation to stalk them, however. Most interviewers generally frown on stalkers.

I know if you're Interviewing for a dream job that you are doing everything you can to put your best foot forward. But remember, the company is also trying to do the same. They want to hide their flaws and zits as much as you want to hide yours. So take advantage of the opportunity to ask them the difficult questions as well.

where can I find a great internship?

Ah, the challenge of the internship. It is one of those Catch 22s in life. In order to get a great job when you graduate, you have to have solid experience, but how do you get solid experience without having a good job in the first place? In order to solve this great mystery, let me introduce you to my good friend, and soon to be yours, "internship."

An internship is a great opportunity for you to not only gain valuable experience in an industry, but also to essentially "test drive" a career path to see if it is something you want to pursue. On top of that, most college degree programs require that you have completed an internship prior to graduating.

Before you even begin to search for an internship opportunity, evaluate what you're looking for. If you don't know what you want in an internship, how will you ever know if you've found it? (That's deep, I know.) Figure out if you desire to gain some specific skills, work for a certain company, have a unique experience, or simply to fulfill a college requirement. Once you've taken the time to answer the "why" part of the equation, then it is time to answer the "how." Here are some resources to find that killer internship you're looking for:

school / career counselors
Sometimes I wonder if school counselors were once part of the CIA - they have contacts with everybody. Even the organizations and companies that you think are impossible to get hooked up with, your counselor knows a guy who knows a guy who can get you in. It's crazy, I know. Sit down with your counselor or advisor in high school or college and discuss what it is that you're looking for and see where that takes you.

your network
When I say "your network," I'm talking about all the connections you have with people from friends to family to teachers to that strange guy you met on the Internet. When you talk with other people in your network about opportunities you're looking for, you'll be amazed at what you find. Maybe you have a friend who is in a similar internship that you're interested in who might be able to get you in. Maybe a relative or a family friend works at an organization that sounds appealing. All around you are opportunities for incredible internships, but you have to let your network know what you're after.

the power of the web
In the digital age that we live, the Internet is an effective, but often overlooked method for finding internships. Go online and search, not just "internships," but specifically a description of what you're looking for or companies that fit your criteria.

Once you have a list of several internship possibilities that seem attractive, go back through the process like you did when deciding on a college. Compare the pros and cons of each option and see where you land.

chapter forty-one
my boss is a jerk... should I quit?

Just because your boss is a jerk doesn't mean you need to storm out today and go slash his tires. That may not be the smartest thing in the world. Throughout your working career, you will probably have several different bosses, and you'll find that each one is different. Some are certainly easier to work for than others, but if you quit a job every time someone is a jerk to you, you'll end up having a "bagillion" different jobs over your lifetime. (That's a lot of jobs if you're unclear on how much a "bagillion" is.)

While I know finding a new job always seems like a good option if you're in a bad situation with your boss, here are some questions to consider before you jump ship:

do you like your job?
This is a critical question to ask, because if you are doing a job that you hate, you're always going to be miserable. I'm a huge believer in doing something that you love, so you should ask yourself if you really enjoy what you're doing. If you love what you're doing and the people you work with, but hate your boss, then you need to determine how big of a deal the boss is to the

entire equation. If you hate what you're doing already and your boss just contributes to that, then you should begin to explore some other options.

is this a phase or is this the way it is?

Before you jump to any conclusions about your boss, it is important to ask yourself this question. Every business and industry has seasons or periods of time that are busier and more stressful than others. If you're an accountant, tax time in April may cause a little extra stress. If you're in retail, the period from Thanksgiving to Christmas is slightly insane. If every business has ebbs and flows, assume that your boss has them as well. In addition, as much as we try to separate work and home life, if your boss is having issues in her personal life, it will definitely affect her mood at the office. If this is the case, try to cut her some slack instead of just bailing on her.

is the timing right?

One of my favorite sayings is "the right thing at the wrong time is still the wrong thing." You should consider if the timing is right when you are considering making a transition out of your current job. It may make more sense for you to wait a few months before making a change. Think through what your new job options may be. It would be wise to have something lined up before you leave. Also, consider where you are financially and how much you have set aside in your emergency fund. Take several factors into consideration before making a move you may later regret.

what are your other options?

Quitting with no clue of what comes next is not a good plan. Before you quit, consider what your other options may be. Can you be transferred to a different department? Can your responsibilities be changed so you don't have to deal with that boss as much? What else can you do before you just quit? And if you do decide to quit, make sure you have a game plan in place first. What is your plan B? Where will you work instead and how soon will you be able to start?

If you do end up leaving a job for any reason, here are a few things to remember on your way out:

finish strong

It doesn't matter how much you hate your job, your boss, or your co-workers, you still have the responsibility to finish strong. You should work as hard on your last day as you did on your first day. Leave an impression, preferably a positive one. This means not calling in sick for your last day!

don't burn bridges

You have no idea what the future holds for you. For all you know, you may be back at this same company in a few years. On top of that, you may need a reference or recommendation from this boss or company in the future, so do not stab them in the back.

take the high road

Regardless of how the boss or anyone else treats you on your way out, take the high road. There is no need to sling mud or to waste your breath on her if she is acting like a jerk to you. Be mature so that you can leave with your head held high.

Before you make any snap decision and quit on a whim, first take a deep breath and think things through. It is always a good idea to get some advice from someone you trust who may be older and wiser than you (i.e. Your parents – even though "they don't know anything!"). Also, take a few days, or even a week or two, before making any type of decision. One day you may feel like quitting but the next day you may feel fine. (Maybe you just had some indigestion from the all-you-can-eat buffet you ate at the night before.)

the future:
swimming in the deep end

chapter forty-two
who am I?

For centuries, people have struggled to find their identity and answer the question, "Who am I?" You would think it would be easy to figure out, but perhaps it is simply part of the journey of life. Human beings will go to great lengths to answer this question. People read books, seek psychics, solicit input, and take trips to find themselves.

Yet we continue to live with this ongoing identity crisis. Often times we live life as if we are a part of a masquerade. We wear masks to disguise and cover who we really are for fear of what others will think about us. We worry that if people know who we really are, they won't like us or will think less of us. We end up trying to find our identities in other people, places, and things only to be left feeling empty inside. The journey to finding your own identity and answering the question, "Who am I?" is a continual part of life. Here are some ideas to consider as you take this journey:

if you don't determine your identity, others will determine it for you

In our culture, it is easy to get sucked into the trap of letting others determine your identity for you. You know as well as I do that this is a major challenge in school because of the labels and stereotypes that get attached to people. Peer pressure is a real battle, and it is very easy to conform and go with the crowd. But until you begin to stand up for yourself, choose what you will and won't do, and decide who you are and who you're not, people will walk all over you. If you allow that to happen, then you will have allowed other people to determine your identity for you. Standing up for yourself and determining your identity comes with consequences both positive and negative. When you determine your identity and who you are as a person, you might lose friends, status or popularity. But when you establish who you are as a person, you will have more confidence and a stronger sense of self-worth.

your identity is not determined by people or stuff

It is extremely easy to attempt to find your identity in a relationship, a group of people, or possessions. But none of these things determine your value. Maybe you've seen this happen before: after a breakup, some guys and girls are not even sure how to function independently of the other person because so much of their identities were wrapped up in that relationship. Or the students who are consumed with their appearances and always think they are too fat, too skinny, too tall, or too short. They are obsessed with their looks or having the right clothes, and their entire identity is consumed by something superficial. How many adults do you know whose entire identities are built upon their work and their career? As we stated in chapter 33, who you are is more important than what you do. Your identity is not found in a relationship, what you drive, where you live, what your grades are, the clothes you wear, how you look, the way you talk, or who your friends are. Period.

ask those closest to you

Talk with those people in your life who love you the most, and ask them how they see you as a person. With this in mind, let me again stress the previous point that your identity is not found in what other people think of you. Often times we look at this in a negative light, but it can also be extremely positive when you talk with the people in your life who love you for you. These are people such as your parents, siblings, close friends, teachers, and others in your life that genuinely know and care about you. Ask them how they see you. Often times they have the ability to see what you don't, and may even see the potential in you that has been overlooked.

answer the question: who am I not?

A great way to begin to determine your identity and answer the question "Who am I?" is to ask the opposite question "Who am I not?" This is generally a simpler question to answer, because it is easier to identify those things that don't represent who we are. Use a question like this as a springboard to then be able to answer the original question, "Who am I?"

Quite honestly, I don't know if it's possible to ever arrive at a complete and solid answer to this question. We are living, breathing organisms, and who we are as individuals is continually evolving, changing, and growing. While that may be the case, continue to strive to answer this question. Your life will continue to change, but do the hard work to discover the core and foundation of who you are as a person.

what matters most?

One thing we commonly fail to do is take the time to truly determine what our priorities are. We each have a sense of what matters most in our lives, but is the way we're living life actually matching up with what we say our priorities are? In some cases yes, but in many cases, the answer is no. When determining what matters most to you, here are some principles to consider:

everybody is different

If we made a list of the different priorities or things that matter most to students, we would have a wide range of items on the list. We would have priorities such as family, health, money, recreation, quality of life, education, sports, friends, and work, just to name a few. But if we had students rank what mattered most to them, everyone's list would be different. Why? Because what is important to you may not be as important to me and vice versa. It can be very easy to let the priorities of others influence how we decide what's important to us. When you see someone with lots of wealth and the lifestyle to prove it, it is easy to gravitate towards those priorities because it looks appealing. But if those priorities go against the grain of who you are as a person, you will constantly be in conflict. It doesn't matter what is important to your friends, your family, or anyone else. You have to determine what matters most and what is important to you.

priorities evolve & change
Answering the question, what matters most, is a constant process throughout life. When you were in elementary school, your priorities were playing at recess, sniffing colored markers, and not getting picked last in gym. Today, I'm sure your priorities are slightly different. (Well, except for the marker sniffing habit you're still trying to kick.) The truth is, when you graduate and you're out on your own, you may have a new set of priorities that you try to live by. Often times, priorities can be dictated by your stage in life. If you're in college, education and studying may be a top priority at the time, but that will obviously change when you graduate. If you're single and trying to climb the corporate ladder, your priorities will likely be completely different than if you were married with three kids.

too many priorities will paralyze you
It can be easy to have a lot of things that are important to you and, as a result, you end up being pulled in several directions. The danger is that you can try to do everything and be everything, but you end up accomplishing nothing. As I've stated before, we all have limits, and there is only so much that we can do. Some of the most successful businesses and companies are those that do one thing and do it really well.

the major priority indicators
If you're having a difficult time determining what matters most to you, the two best indicators for your priorities are your time and your money. Check out your schedule for the past month and look over your checkbook, and you will quickly get a sense of what matters most to you. If you're big into clothes and fashion, you will be able to tell that by looking at your time and money. If school and education are a major priority for you, your calendar and checkbook will reflect that. With that

in mind, once you determine and establish your priorities, continually keep an eye on your time and your money to make sure that what is important to you is matching up with how you're living.

By determining what matters most in your life, you are setting a framework for how you will live on a daily basis. Your priorities will help determine where you live, what kind of work you do, and even who your friends are. It can have a trickledown effect that will influence every element of your life. Because of this, recognize and realize just how important it is to not only determine what matters most to you, but also to be proactive in how you live that out.

how do I find my purpose in life?

This is the age old question of, "Why am I here?" Unfortunately, too often students feel like they have no purpose, meaning, or direction, and as result, they can wander aimlessly through life. In a deeper way, some students feel if they have no purpose or meaning, then there is no point to life. As a result, the depressing reality is that suicide is the third leading cause of death for teenagers.[1] This is extremely tragic because every single human life has meaning, purpose, and value. Regardless of your background or belief system, we all have purpose. Even if you don't believe you have a purpose, not believing in it doesn't make it go away. In the same way, just by believing that the Earth has no gravity doesn't mean I'm going to float into outer space.

Before you begin to answer the question of finding purpose, you have to first define what "purpose" is and isn't. Dictionary. com defines purpose as "the reason for which something exists or is done, made, used, etc." So then it seems that purpose is defined by the creator or origin of something. For example, if I create some type of contraption or device, then as the creator of the item, isn't it my responsibility to determine its purpose? Without getting into a spiritual or theological debate, finding your purpose involves asking the question, where did I come from? Personally, I believe humans were created by a loving God, and that He is involved in our daily lives. So for me, purpose and meaning stems largely from that belief.

One of the best pieces of advice I've heard regarding finding your purpose in life is to let your life speak. By this I mean, what is it in life that you are truly passionate about? What is it that you are naturally drawn to? What is it that moves you emotionally or breaks your heart? A great way to see this in action is to watch a group of children. Little kids are too young to fully comprehend all that is going on around them and probably aren't asking questions about purpose and identity quite yet. But there are some things in life that they are just naturally drawn to more than others. There are some things they have natural skill, talent, or ability in. It may be that they are drawn to helping others. Or they are naturally compassionate. Or they have a certain sense of justice and fairness when it comes to sharing or getting along with others. Think back to your childhood. What were the qualities and characteristics of your early years? These memories may hold the key to answering the deeper question of purpose for you.

As you search out meaning and reason for existence, let me encourage you to be patient. We live in a "microwave" culture that is looking for a quick fix or an easy answer. When it comes to determining one's purpose in life, it is not an overnight process. It takes weeks, months, and even years of searching and asking, seeking and discovering what your purpose looks like. As we've covered throughout the book, that looks different for everyone. One person's purpose may be complete confusion to another person.

In addition, purpose, like priorities, evolves over time. You may feel that your sole purpose right now is to do well in school and graduate. Or to make a difference in the lives of others. Or to restrain from beating up your little brother. All of which are noble. Because purpose evolves over time, that tells us something: we don't have to know all the answers today. It is easy to get so consumed by trying to know all the details, and ins and outs of life, that we miss out on life itself. While I certainly wouldn't recommend avoiding this question altogether, I would also recommend not going to the other extreme and getting so caught up in it that life passes you by.

So what's the purpose of your life? I'm not sure that I have the perfect answer for you. I guess if I did, I should charge more for this book! But that's part of the journey of life. As I was beginning to write this book, I came across a quote that fits well here. E.L. Doctorow once said that "Writing is like driving a car at night. You can see only as far as your headlights, but you can make the whole trip that way. You don't have to see where you're going, you don't have to see your destination or everything you will pass along the way. You just have to see two or three feet ahead of you." The same thing is true with life. You may not have all the answers or fully understand everything now, but if you can see a few feet in front of you, you can make the entire journey.

Finding work that you are **passionate** about, good at, and enjoy is one of the most **important** things you can do right now.

what should I do when I grow up?

Several years ago when you were just a little tike, this was a fun question to kick around, wasn't it? One day you wanted to be a firefighter. The next day you wanted to be a cheerleader. You considered being a doctor. You even tossed out the idea of being a space cowboy, but then you decided maybe not. It was fun to consider all your various options as a child, because every day you could be something different. But now you're on the verge of having to actually answer that question, and, like me, you may be finding that it is not as easy to answer as you had hoped.

There are countless options of what you can be and what you can do, but really keying in on that one career path is a challenge. Let me provide you with a couple of broad principles to consider as you try to determine what you want to be when you grow up:

don't pick something for the money
It is far too common that people make career path decisions based on where they think the money is. Do you know how many doctors and lawyers there are who may be doing well

financially but absolutely hate what they do? Life is too short to do something just for a paycheck. If you have to work to make a living, wouldn't you rather do something you enjoy? In my opinion, if you do something well enough, people will pay you for it.

As an example, I read an article recently about a guy who was making a six-figure income as a corporate lawyer in New York. The problem was that he didn't really enjoy what he did and truly lacked passion for his work. He decided what he was really passionate about and always wanted to do was play with LEGOs (Yes, you read that correctly.). You remember those little building blocks from your childhood? So today, the guy gets paid crazy money to build sculptures, designs, and pieces of art out of LEGOs! If you do what you love and do it well enough, someone will pay you for it.

pick a career for you, not your family

Maybe in your family, there has been some type of "generational career" that several members of your family have done. Perhaps there is a family business that you are feeling pressured to be a part of. But just like those who follow the money, you need to find work that *you* are passionate about, not what your parents think you should do for a living. If you have a family business you want to be a part of, then great, but don't do something just because you feel you have to or because you're supposed to.

don't stress about which industry offers a "hot" career

Every year there is a new "hot" industry that offers a ridiculous amount of hype by promising unlimited income potential, endless growth, opportunity, and blah, blah, blah. I'm sure they don't promote offering "blah," but that is what most of it is. If you spend your life trying to find what the "hot" industry is, you will be bouncing around for the rest of your life. In the late 1990's, there was the Dot-Com Boom, and the hot thing was to have some type of e-commerce website. It became a modern day gold rush, but today most of the "companies" that were started during that time are no longer even in business.

consider how long your working life will be

I remember for me, I felt a huge stress because I thought that whatever I decided to do after college would be what I would do for the rest of my life. But in reality, nothing could be further from the truth. Think about it. If you start your career at age 22 and work until you're 65 years old, that means you will work for 43 years! How many adults do you know who have worked at the same job doing the same work for 43 years? Very few. The U.S. Department of Labor estimates that about one in five workers will change jobs every year. They also estimate that each generation will average more job moves and career changes than the generation before. That means you will likely change jobs or have more careers than your parents had, and they likely had more job changes than their parents.

So while those are certainly some solid principles to consider when looking at potential job opportunities, what are some criteria that you should be looking for in a career? Here are my top three criteria:

passion

What are you passionate about? For some people, this is a very easy question to answer, but for others, it poses more of a challenge. This was a very difficult question for me, and it certainly took some time and soul searching to figure out the answer. Today, I get paid to do what I love which involves speaking, writing, and making a difference in the lives of others. It is important that you don't confuse passion with enthusiasm. You can be a very mellow, introverted individual and still care passionately about something. Often times we think of passion as people who are slightly crazy and overly energetic to the point it makes you concerned for your safety. But rather, passion is about doing something you love and find meaningful and sharing that passion with the world.

talent

What are you good at? Let's be honest for a second: people don't want to do something they suck at. I like playing sports, but if I'm competing against someone who is killing me, and I'm no good at the game, then it is no fun anymore. People want to do things that they are good at. What is it in your world that has always come naturally to you? You don't have to spend massive amounts of time practicing or working at it. It is just something that you've always been able to do. Maybe it is something with athletics, music, art, problem solving, or even your compassion for others. If you have to work, wouldn't you rather do something you're good at? It'll make your job a heck of a lot easier!

enjoyment

What do you like to do? Again, if you have to make a living doing something, wouldn't you rather do something that you enjoy? Unfortunately, though, so many people live their lives with the mentality of "Thank God, it's Friday" to "Oh God, it's Monday." Think back to the LEGO guy I mentioned earlier...do you really think he dreads Monday mornings? Probably not, because he is doing something he loves. Now don't get me wrong. Just because you are doing something that you are passionate about, you are good at, and you like to do, doesn't mean that you will enjoy every minute of the day. With every job, regardless of how much you like it, there are elements that come with the territory that you may not enjoy as much.

Finding work that you are passionate about, that you are good at, and that you like to do is one of the most important things you can do right now. When you consider how much of your life you will spend doing some type of work, it just seems logical that you would spend the time to find something that you love.

what should I do now to prepare for tomorrow?

Life after high school can seem a little overwhelming and stressful and with everything that we have covered, it seems difficult to even know where to start. But you have to start somewhere, right? Sometimes we think if we just get started and do something, eventually we'll get where we want to go. In reality, that's probably not the best way to get anywhere.

Think about it this way. Let's say you are in New York City, and you decide to drive to Los Angeles. A nice little road trip, to say the least (2,776 miles to be exact). Do you think the smartest thing to do will be to just get in your car and start driving west? You know that Los Angeles is west of New York City, so you figure if you just drive until you hit another ocean, then you'll be close. This is probably not very effective or efficient though, huh? Instead, before you even get into your car, what if you take the time to check out a map for some directions, or maybe go online and get an opinion from Google or MapQuest. I think we would all agree that your trip would go a little smoother if you had a plan. The same thing is true with your life.

Take the time to create a plan. Answer the questions of "Where do I want to be in one year? Five years? Ten years?" Once you have at least an idea of where you are going, then you can begin to think backwards to determine what you need to do to get there. For example, if you want to have your own business as an interior decorator, that won't just magically happen because you want it to. You have to create a plan for what you will need to do to get there. I will talk more about creating and following goals in the next chapter, but understand that goals are a critical part of preparing for tomorrow.

As it relates to creating and following a plan, it's also important to be proactive. Again, rarely will you actually end up where you want to be just by accident. You have to be proactive in determining not only where you're going, but also how you're going to get there. The more intentional you are about planning ahead, the more you increase your chances of accomplishing those goals.

In addition, you should have flexibility within your plan. If you got a map from Google for your directions from New York to Los Angeles, but part way there you run into some road construction, does that mean you have bad directions, and you should just toss them out? Of course not. It just means you hit construction which is part of the drive. Stick to your plan of what you need to do today to accomplish your dream tomorrow, but allow room for flexibility and changes. If there is a major change in your life, then it will certainly affect how you are going to accomplish your goals. But there is no need to completely toss the dream out the window.

The other thing you should do now to prepare for tomorrow is dream. And dream big. Not in a corny, cheesy way with rainbows, butterflies, and unicorns, but truly dream what you want your life to be in the next several years. People get where they want to go in life because they planned on getting there. Dream big, and imagine what your life could be like in the next few years. Ask yourself questions like:

If I knew I couldn't fail, what would I attempt?
If I had an endless amount of money, what would I do with it?
What would my ideal life look like?

Begin to think these things through now, so you end up where you want to go on purpose. Figuring out where to start can seem like an overwhelming and daunting task. But if you create a plan for where you want to be, then you will have a road map for how you're going to get there.

how do I create goals?

Creating and working towards goals are critical components of being successful in the future. Goals are a way for you to bring clarity and focus to where you're going in life. There's the old saying that "If you aim at nothing, you will hit it every time." There are three basic components to creating and carrying out your goals:

establish priorities
Before you can do anything, you have to determine what is most important to you. Once you have clarity on what your priorities are, then you can establish how that affects your time, your money, and everything else around you. I discussed this more in depth in the earlier chapter, "What matters most?" so refer back to that if you still have questions about establishing priorities.

build goals around priorities
Once you have established what your priorities are, then it's time to begin actually organizing your schedule and your life around those things. Begin to create a list of goals that are based on your priorities. Here's what I mean: If your family is

your top priority, then what goals do you need to establish in order to reflect that? If school is your top priority, what goals will help you to reflect that? As you begin to create goals based on your priorities, here is an acronym for the criteria your goals should meet – S.M.A.R.T. Goals:

specific

What is the exact result you want to achieve? Be as specific as possible. Goals like "I want to make more money" sound nice but are really vague. By answering specifically how much money you want to make, you can be more detailed when setting your goal. For example, you could say, "I want to make $10,000 in the next 6 months." That is a very specific, detailed goal.

measurable

What is a successful result? How will you know that you've reached your goal? For example, if I said "I want to have a closer relationship with my mom," that's good, but how do you measure that? How do you know if you're accomplishing it? Try to make it measurable. So instead you could say this, "I want to spend two hours hanging out with my mom one night each week." Now you can measure that. You can track how you're doing. You're working to accomplish the same thing as your original goal of "I want to have a closer relationship with my mom," but now you can measure it.

attainable

I'm all for dreaming big, but you have to ask yourself if your goal is realistic. "I want to be the first junior high student to play in the NBA" – sounds good; it's even measurable and specific, but I don't know how attainable it is. You have to balance between pushing yourself to accomplish a challenging goal but also making it realistic.

relevant

How does achieving this goal align with your priorities? If you say, "I want to be a millionaire by the time I'm 25," that's great, but how does that goal tie back into your priorities? If none of your priorities have anything to do with money or financial independence, then the goal is not relevant. Your goals must be relevant to your priorities.

time

What is your cut-off date for achieving this goal? There should be a set finish line, so you are pushing yourself to achieve your goal. Without a timeline for accomplishing the goal, it is very easy to get off track, and you just get to it when you get to it. A goal without a deadline is just a wish.

write it down

Your goals must be written down. When you write down your goal, what you want to accomplish not only becomes clearer, it becomes a visual reminder of what you're trying to do. When you write it down, you are making a commitment with yourself. It's more than a mental goal that can change based on circumstances.

make it happen

Now it's time to transfer those goals over into your schedule. Let's think through an average week in the life of a student to help create a game plan for accomplishing goals. Once you have established your goals, you need to create some specific steps in order to accomplish those goals. For example, if you want to raise $1,000 for charity at your next club fundraiser, that won't just happen on its own; will it? You may need to create a checklist of things that need to happen. Your list may be to call local businesses for support, brainstorm ideas to raise money, talk with friends to get them involved, etc. You need to create a list of tasks that must get done in order to accomplish that bigger goal.

Now that you have a list of items and tasks that you need to be working on in order to accomplish your goal, you will want to actually schedule in your planner when you will do those tasks. When you create a schedule and a plan, you are taking time to save time. Block out realistic amounts of time to accomplish specific tasks and follow through with your game plan.

Throughout the entire process of creating and carrying out your goals, continue to do two things: constant evaluation and intense focus. Continually look at your schedule to make sure that your priorities are reflecting how you spend your time. If they're not and everything seems out of whack, make some changes so your schedule truly reflects your priorities. On top of all this, stay focused on your goals. Remember the bigger picture of why you're doing what you're doing.

what do I need to do to be successful?

This depends on what you think is "successful." To some people, success is having lots of money. To others, success is having lots friends or being famous. And to others, success is being a good spouse or a good parent. What does success look like to you? In order to know what you need to be successful, you have to consider what success means to you. Otherwise, how will you ever know if you are successful?

In sports, there are ways to score points and keep score so you know if you are being successful or not. In basketball, if there were no baskets and all you did was dribble the ball around, how would you ever know if you are being successful or not? But, again, the nice thing about life is you get to determine what success looks like for you.

Regardless of how you would define success, here are some common characteristics of "successful" people:

passionate
Successful people are passionate, not just about the work they do in their career, but about life in general. Again, passion

doesn't mean that you get up every morning and do jumping jacks with Richard Simmons just for the heck of it (On a side note, doesn't that guy just give you the creeps?!). It just means you genuinely love life and how you are living it.

hard worker

It is easy to look at movie stars, professional athletes, and other culturally "successful" people, and assume everything they have was just handed to them on a silver platter. While that may be the case with some, most people who are successful have worked their butts off. Think about it with the Olympics. These people work for years spending countless hours to prepare for their events which may be over in, literally, a matter of seconds. It is the unseen hours of hard work that help them be successful when that brief moment arrives.

lifelong learner

Did you know that the average millionaire reads one non-fiction book every month? These are people we would consider to be successful, yet they are still not content with where they are. They are continually striving to learn something new. In today's world, you are paid less for what you do and more for what you know. The more you know, the more valuable you become. No one who is considered successful believes that learning and education end after you graduate. It's only the beginning. Sorry to depress you.

disciplined

While this may come easier to some than others, if you're going to be successful in life, you have to learn to be disciplined. Being disciplined doesn't mean you must have every minute of every day completely planned out. But, then again, organizationally, you can't be a complete disaster. Working hard, being a lifelong learner, accomplishing goals – everything we've talked about – requires discipline. Create your game plan and then execute it. I don't mean kill it, just carry it out (some of you will get that joke later).

persistent

Anytime you are trying to accomplish something of significance you are going to run into a variety of challenges, barriers, and obstacles that make it difficult to keep going. But in order to be successful, you can't just give up when the going gets tough. You have to be willing to keep fighting and giving it everything you've got before throwing in the towel. At the same time, you have to be smart enough to choose where you will be your best. If you're five feet tall and your dream is to play in the NBA, but you've never picked up a basketball, it may be time to begin pursuing other options. Just a thought.

sacrifice to win

In order to achieve any goal, you have to learn to make sacrifices along the way. Nobody in his right mind eats healthy and exercises just for the fun of it. These people make those sacrifices because they know that is what it takes to win physically. I love the quote that says, "Do what you have to do so you get to do what you want to do." That is an excellent description of how successful people live life.

Although success may be a relative and subjective term that means something different to everyone, anyone who would be considered successful has the majority of these characteristics and qualities. The idea of an "overnight success" is just a myth that people get sucked into believing. If you want to succeed, start right now where you are, set goals of what being a "success" looks like for you, then work your butt off to get there.

how can I make a
difference in this world?

Deep down we all have the desire and dream to do more than live an average, boring, mundane existence. We desire to truly live life and make a difference in the lives of others. We want to do more than go through the motions of life. Each of us dreams of making a real impact and leaving a legacy. Maybe you feel like this. Or maybe it is the leftover pizza you ate that is talking to you. Or gas. Of course the gas may be caused by the leftover pizza. Wow, my A.D.D. has gotten the best of me, and we have really veered off track.

Making a difference seems like one of those nice pie-in-the-sky dreams, but it doesn't always feel very realistic. Maybe you think you are just a teenager or young adult, and there is nothing you could personally do that would make a difference. But you have an opportunity, just like anyone else, to do something and be something that makes a difference. Here are some ideas to get you started:

think of *your* world before *the* world
Often times when we talk about making a difference, we think in terms of saving the whales, feeding the hungry, curing

diseases or hugging a tree. But when you begin to think about making a difference in the world it can seem overwhelming. Personally, I'm no Mother Teresa, so making a difference like she did seems nearly impossible for someone like me. But making a difference goes beyond what we think of on a global scale. It means, before you can make a difference in *the* world, you have to first make a difference in *your* world. Where is your world? It is your neighborhood, your family, your school, your friends, your job, and any other place that you live life. You have the greatest opportunity to do something in your world, so start right where you're at.

start small & simple
Again, we can get so consumed with doing something on such a large and grand scale that we miss out on the simplest, and sometimes most effective, ways to make a difference. You don't have to have millions of dollars or be best friends with Oprah to do something significant. Sometimes some of the best ways to make a difference are the things that are free. Think about it this way. What are some of the most memorable Christmas gifts you have ever received? Almost always, the things that are the most memorable aren't the items that cost the most but rather had the most thought put into them. Simple things like writing a friend an encouraging note, picking up trash at your school, or simply telling your parents thanks. Man, that would freak them out, wouldn't it?! It is not always the big things that matter. Sometimes it is just small and simple that makes the biggest impact.

do something
It is easy to get so consumed by thinking through how we can make the biggest difference that we end up doing nothing. On top of that, it is easy to live with the mentality of "someday" when it comes to making a difference. You may think at your age there isn't anything of significance that you can do, but nothing could be further from the truth. If you always wait until "someday" arrives before you do something to make a difference, you'll end up never doing anything. When it comes

to making a difference, doing something is almost always better than doing nothing.

be a part of something bigger than you

I know there are certain things, as an individual, I can do to make a difference, but, at the same time, I want to be part of something that is bigger than me. As I've stated before, we all have limits and a capacity for what we can do. As humans, there is only so much we can do before we reach our limit. But when we're a part of something that is bigger than ourselves, now we're able to do so much more collectively than any one of us could do individually. Look for groups, clubs, and organizations that you can join to partner with others in making a difference.

In life, you can make a lot of money and be famous, have a corner office and a fancy job title, drive new cars and live in big mansions, but what does all that mean when you die? Nothing really. But if you make a difference in the life of someone else, that is something that lives on. Whether you realize it or not, every day you are making a difference in the lives of others, either positively or negatively. Recognize and realize that you are making a difference today.

how do I make the most of my life?

This is a great question that you really have to think through and answer for yourself. Not for your friend. Not for your parents. Not for that strange kid you share a locker with who sniffs glue. But for you. You need to determine how you can make the most of your life. Success in life is very subjective, and what is considered to be a successful life to one person may not be as important to someone else. Consider questions like these:

When you die, how do you want to be remembered?
What do you want people to say about you at your funeral?
If you thought your life was a complete failure,
what would that look like?

If you asked 100 students these questions, you would get 100 different answers. But by answering these questions for yourself, you begin to get a better sense of how you can make the most of your life. With that in mind, here are some principles that I strive to live by in order to make the most of my life.

enjoy the journey
In the busyness and chaos that is life, it is very easy to get so bogged down in everything that you forget to enjoy the journey. Live each day to its fullest, and don't let a moment pass by. Remember those days in kindergarten with recess, nap time, and cheap milk? Those days are gone, unfortunately. Each year as you get a little older (and perhaps add a few pounds) are you taking the time to smell the roses and enjoy the journey?

try something new
In life, it is very easy to live on the sidelines and always play it safe. We get into ruts and routines and rarely step outside the box to take a risk and try something new. Mix it up in your life to break the routines every now and then. Order something different than the usual dish. Go a different route to work. Turn off the TV for a week. Take a road trip with friends. Learn a new language or skill. Try something new.

you've got one life to live
At some point, all of our lives are going to come to an end. Regardless of your belief about what happens after that, you have one chance to live the life you have right now. As I write this, it is 11:28 a.m., Tuesday, May 27, 2008. Never again will I live in this moment of time. So if I've got one life to live, then I don't want to waste a second of it. Ask yourself, "Is this the best use of this moment?"

live with no regrets
There are two main types of regret. The things we do that we wish we had not done, and the things we did not do that we wish we had done. We have all done those stupid things we regret doing and will probably continue to do them throughout life. But I'm talking about not missing out on opportunities that we will one day wish we had taken a chance at. I would rather be involved with a train wreck and know at least I tried, than to look back someday and wonder, "What if?"

do what you love, love what you do

As we mentioned in chapter 45, we all have to work to make a living, so, personally, I would rather do something I love. Something that is more than a job or a paycheck, but something with meaning and value. Right now I get paid to do what I love, and I can't imagine life any other way.

live on purpose

We discussed this in an earlier chapter, but to reiterate, nobody gets anywhere by accident. Your life isn't an accident, and you are not a mistake. Your life has purpose, meaning, and value so you should live accordingly.

These are just a few of the things that you can do to make the most of your life. Don't wait another moment to make the most of your life. You are this age only once, so start living a life that you are proud of and that you are living on purpose.

now what?

One of my favorite questions in the world is two simple words:

Now What?

This is such a critical question because it allows us the opportunity to do something differently based on what we've learned. How often have you heard an idea, read a book, listened to a talk, or been inspired to do something different in your life only to end up doing nothing? We're all guilty of it so rather than learning just for the sake of learning, what are you going to do differently to implement what you've learned? Otherwise, what's the point? If you have no plans to apply anything you read, then there is no reason to read in the first place.

If we do things the way we've always done, we're going to continue to get the same results. That seems like common sense. If you do things the way you've always done and yet expect different results, it is insanity! It makes sense, right? So again, we come back to the question, what are you going to do differently as a result of what you've read?

As I stated in the introduction, I have no magic formula, secret pill, or special sauce that is going to change or revolutionize your life. What is going to change your life is YOU. At the risk of sounding corny or clichéd, the fact is you have the ability to make your life anything that you want it to be. Regardless of your background, your family, your personality, your education, your status, or any other excuses you can come up with, you hold the power to your own destiny.

I would challenge you not only to begin to implement and apply some of these ideas into your everyday life, but also to encourage other students to do the same. If you've read something that has caused you to think or do things differently, then chances are, it would have the same effect on other students. One of the best ways that humans learn and retain information is by teaching others.

So again, not only ask yourself the question, but make a commitment that you are going to do something differently in your life. What you do from here is entirely up to you.

Now What?

Welcome to your Reality Check.

Should I go to college?
1. http://www.usatoday.com/money/perfi/college/2006-06-11-debt-cover-usat_x.htm
2. http://www.freemoneyfinance.com/2006/11/college_degree_.html
3. http://www.cnn.com/2006/US/Careers/02/24/cb.no.degree.jobs/index.html

Are the ACT and the SAT really that important?
1. www.math.com/students/kaplan/satoract.html
2. www.math.com/students/kaplan/satoract.html

How do you apply for college?
1. http://www.ivysuccess.com/admissions_stats_2008.html

How am I going to pay for college?
1. http://www.usatoday.com/money/perfi/college/2006-06-11-debt-cover-usat_x.htm
2. Calculations by the Project on Student Debt from the National Center for Education Statistics (NCES), National Postsecondary Student Aid Study (NPSAS), 1993 and 2004 undergraduates, Data Analysis System (DAS).
3. Trends in Student Aid, The College Board, 2006
4. http://moneycentral.msn.com/content/CollegeandFamily/Cutcollegecosts/P108589.asp

What should I major in?
1. http://media.www.thehilltoponline.com/media/storage/paper590/news/2006/03/31/Campus/College.Students.Change.Career.Paths.As.Often.As.They.Change-1775476.shtml

SEX: If I love someone, why not?
1. http://www.msnbc.msn.com/id/23574940/
2. The Kaiser Family Foundation, Sexually Transmitted Diseases in the United States, Fact Sheet, June 2003.
3. Guttmacher Institute, U.S. Teenage Pregnancy Statistics: National and State Trends and Trends by Race and Ethnicity, 2006, - http://www.guttmacher.org/pubs/fb_sexEd2006.html
4. http://www.frc.org/get.cfm?i=IS06B01

Do I need insurance?
1. http://www.consumeraffairs.com/news04/2005/bankruptcy_study.html

Should I be concerned about identity theft?
1. http://www.zanderins.com/idtheft/stats.aspx

Should I get a credit card?
1. http://www.fool.com/ccc/secrets/secrets.htm
2. http://www.money-zine.com/Financial-Planning/Debt-Consolidation/Credit-Card-Debt-Statistics

How do I avoid screwing up a job interview?
1. http://humor.business-opportunities.biz/2008/03/15/10-worst-job-interview-blunders/
2. http://www.reuters.com/article/lifestyleMolt/idUSSP687020080313?pageNumber=2&virtualBrandChannel=0

How do I find my purpose in life?
1. http://www.teensuicide.us/articles1.html

about the author

Grant Baldwin is an engaging communicator and a leading expert at helping students prepare for life after high school. Grant is a popular youth motivational speaker and also regularly presents at educator conferences. He has given hundreds of presentations and has spoken to over 250,000 people in 42 states through leadership conferences, conventions, school assemblies, and other student events. While Grant does love speaking and inspiring students, he loves his wife and three daughters more. They live in Springfield, Missouri.

For more info, check out www.GrantBaldwin.com.

keep in touch with grant

As you may have figured out by now, I actually really like students. It's strange, I know. But beyond writing a book or speaking at an event, I love talking with students and hearing what I can do to help them be successful in life.

If there is ever anything I can do for you, please don't hesitate to email me or give me a call. If you've got a question, you need some advice, or you just want to let me know what you thought of *Reality Check*, I'd love to hear from you. My email address is Grant@GrantBaldwin.com.

Here are a few other ways to keep in touch with me:

social networks

You can also track me down on various social networking sites. Here are a few links to find where I'm at...

Facebook – www.facebook.com/grantbaldwinfans
Twitter – www.twitter.com/grantbaldwin
YouTube – www.youtube.com/grantbaldwindotcom

e-newsletter

Keep up to date through this newsletter filled with thought-provoking articles, entertaining stories, and my latest happenings and travels. Sign up at www.GrantBaldwin.com.

One last thing before you go. When you finish this book, I would encourage you to pass it on to a friend. Or better yet, just buy all of your friends their own copy! If it meant something to you, it may mean something to someone else. You never know the simple impact you can make by sharing a book!

Your Friend,

Grant

Reality Check: Teacher's Guide

For most of their life, a student's world has been a pretty simple and steady routine. They've always been told where to go, what time to be there, when to sit, when to stand, on and on the list goes. But they're not always prepared for what happens next.

That's why we created the *Reality Check Teacher's Guide*, a turn-key curriculum that will help students prepare for life after high school. Each lesson plan was designed by a team of educators and students to be easy to implement with no training required. Each lesson plan contains the following...

- Student Outcomes
- Time Needed
- Relationship to National Standards
- Concepts
- Procedures
- Assessment (critical-thinking based)
- Materials Needed (includes student worksheets/handouts)
- Additional Resources
- Enrichment Activities

"It's about preparation! To successfully meet the challenging demands of today's society, it is imperative for high school students to become college and career ready. Toward that end, this teacher's guide to Reality Check *is an extremely valuable tool in a teacher's toolkit for guiding students on their pathway toward a successful and meaningful future."*

–Michael Benjamin, Executive Director, National FCCLA
(Family, Career and Community Leaders of America)

THE FOLLOWING TOPICS ARE AVAILABLE AS TEACHER GUIDES, CORRESPONDING WITH THE *REALITY CHECK* CHAPTERS:

Learn more at
www.TeachRealityCheck.com
and download
five free lesson plans!

PRODUCTS+PRICES

TEACHER PACK

5 GUIDES + 30 BOOKS

This package has everything you need to start teaching *Reality Check* in your classroom today.

$449.95 $748.25 **(40% off)**

REALITY CHECK STARTER KIT

1 GUIDE + 1 BOOK

Choose one of the five Teacher Guides to accompany a copy of *Reality Check*, and begin preparing your students for their future.

$55.95 $74.80 **(25% off)**

REALITY CHECK TEACHER GUIDES

5 GUIDES + 1 BOOK

Reality Check Teacher Guides have 50 lesson plans including already prepared and proven assessments, classroom activities, handouts, and discussion questions in an easy-to-follow format.

$159.95 $314.70 **(49% off)**

REALITY CHECK BOOK

In this humerous and relevant book, *Reality Check*, author Grant Baldwin helps students navigate both the challenges and opportunities of the real world in a practical and applicable manner.

$12.95 $14.95 **(13% off)**

ORDERING IN BULK?

QUANTITY	UNIT PRICE
1-10	$12.95
11-100	$11.00
101-250	$10.00
251+	$7.47*

*Half off the retail price!
Standard Retail - $14.95

HOW DO I ORDER?

The best way to order is online at www.GrantBaldwin.com. If you have specific instructions, contact Lisa Klug at 417.773.0989 or email her at lisa@grantbaldwin.com.

Shipping is 6% of your total order with a minimum of $4. We ship USPS.
If you need expedited shipping or international shipping, please contact Lisa.

GRANT BALDWIN
captivate. innovate. motivate.

Speaking Engagements

Grant Baldwin is an engaging communicator and a leading teen expert who is making a significant impact in the lives of students across the country. Grant has delivered over 500 presentations to over 250,000 students in 42 different states. He has a unique ability to capture an audience's attention with comedy and humor, yet still challenge them to think and apply action to their lives. Grant speaks at schools, conferences, conventions, camps, retreats, and other events for students.

In addition to his presentations for students, Grant is also passionate about helping those who work with teenagers. He understands what students need and is able to present it in a way that connects with your adult audience. Whether you are planning an educator's conference, a professional development in-service, or a community event for parents, Grant will meet your objectives as a presenter. He also offers several programs for educators, parents, and community leaders to help apply the concepts of *Reality Check* to the teens in their lives.

"Grant truly took the time to learn about our organization, its members, our challenges, and our hopes. The result was an overwhelmingly positive experience for our members. If you are looking for something different from your next speaker, consider Grant Baldwin. He won't disappoint."

–Kirk Lawson, National BPA Executive Director

For more information or to schedule Grant to speak at your next event, please visit www.GrantBaldwin.com or contact Lisa Klug at 417.773.0989.